COLORING OUTS

D0652096

"A refreshing, insightful, and humorous look at the Christian life without the characteristic stereotyping that takes the joy out of what God intended to be a joyful and authentic journey through life in meaningful relationship with Jesus Christ and our fellow human beings."

—Doug Burleigh, president, Young Life

"John Westfall expresses truth by telling great stories. I appreciate that. This book helped me to learn some of the truth about myself and the way in which I live out the Christian life. I guarantee that this book will prove worth reading."

—Tony Campolo, author of *Wake Up America!*

"Hooray for John Westfall! I think God calls all of us to "color outside the lines" once in a while. I have been doing it for years. We are called to be more than "pew potatoes" (God's frozen chosen). We need more people who are willing to push back the barriers of "religion" and discover the true unpredictable journey of faith. This is a courageous book, a vital book, a daring book— which invites us all to be real. On these pages you will find hope for a more committed and colorful lifestyle—wrapped in unexpected joy."

—Tim Hansel, author of *You Gotta Keep Dancin'* and *Holy Sweat*

"Why do we as Christians so frequently turn a joyous relationship with Christ into techniques, systems, and rules? Unfortunately I've spent a lot of time trying to mold my faith to others' expectations and then feeling like a great failure. This book comes as a delightful invitation to rediscover the adventure and joy of living with Jesus. Thank you, John!"

—Stephen A. Hayner, president, Inter-Varsity Christian Fellowship

"As refreshing as it is profound, as practical as it is personal, John Westfall's book will bring comfort to some readers and correction to others. Its style resounds with verve, its illustrations ring with clarity, and its observations hit home with accuracy. This is a different approach to discipleship—one from which all of Christ's followers will profit."

—David Hubbard, president, Fuller Theological Seminary

"If a stuffy old Brit like me finds invigorating wisdom in this fun-under-the-gun approach to Christian living, I am sure many others will as well."

—J. I. Packer, author of *Knowing God*

"For a lot of people the word "spirituality" is frightening. John Westfall challenges such thinking by offering new ideas, habits and ways of living in joy and in love. John reminds readers that Christ only asks that we trust him in every area of our lives. Accepting, let alone, following Christ is not a program. It is a relationship."

—Harold Ivan Smith, author of *Positively Single*

"John Westfall knits honesty, wit and wisdom into his tender tapestry of our spiritual foolishness. I found myself in every chapter, and it hurt. I found hope there too, and it healed. A terrific book."

—Lewis B. Smedes, author of *Forgive & Forget*

"With personal vulnerability and wit, John Westfall provides a healing and empowering perspective for people seeking to understand what it means to be in a relationship with Jesus Christ in today's world of high expectations and competing definitions of spirituality."

—Walter C. Wright, president, Regent College

Coloring Outside the Lines

Coloring Outside the Lines

DISCIPLESHIP FOR THE "UNDISCIPLINED"

John Westfall

HarperSanFrancisco
A Division of HarperCollinsPublishers

Grateful acknowledgment is made to the following for permission to reprint material copyrighted or controlled by them:

"Nobody Wins," by Kris Kristofferson, © 1972 by Refca Music Publishing Co. All rights controlled and administered by EMI Blackwood Music Inc. All rights reserved. International copyright secured. Used by permission.

"Jesus Was a Capricorn," by Kris Kristofferson, © 1972 by Refca Music Publishing Co. All rights controlled and administered by EMI Blackwood Music Inc. All rights reserved. International copyright secured. Used by permission.

Credits continue on page 173.

COLORING OUTSIDE THE LINES: *Discipleship for the "Undisciplined."* © 1991 by John Westfall. All rights reserved. Printed in the United States of America. No part of this book may be used or reproduced in any manner whatsoever without written permission except in the case of brief quotations embodied in critical articles and reviews. For information address HarperCollins Publishers, 10 East 53rd Street, New York, NY 10022.

FIRST EDITION

Library of Congress Cataloging-in-Publication Data

Westfall, John.
    Coloring outside the lines : discipleship for the "undisciplined"
    John Westfall.—1st ed.
        p.   cm.
    ISBN 0-06-069298-7
    1. Christian life—1960-   2. Christian life—Presbyterian authors.
    I. Title.
    BV4501.2.W4353   1991
    248.4—dc20   90-55763
                                                               CIP

91 92 93 94 95 HAD 10 9 8 7 6 5 4 3 2 1

This edition is printed on acid-free paper that meets the American National Standards Institute Z39.48 Standard.

This book is dedicated with love to Eileen Alice Westfall who looks beyond the surface and won't settle for less than God's best. Throughout our marriage she has seen me at my best and at my worst and somehow loves me regardless.

and

To Damian Drew Westfall, our son. He has brought me joy, excitement, and great pride. Thank you for mixing such bright colors on the palette of our lives.

CONTENTS

FOREWORD

Do you remember the delightful children's story "The Emperor's New Clothes"? In it, a couple of con men disguised as tailors sell the king a suit of clothes that supposedly are visible only to good and moral people. Of course, there were no clothes. None of the citizens dare to confess that they cannot see the new finery, and so the pretense goes on. The hoax ends when a little boy sees the king walking through the town and blurts out, "He's naked!"

From time to time a book emerges in the Christian world that, in the same direct manner, tells it like it is. My old friend Keith Miller wrote such a book years ago, entitled *The Taste of New Wine*, in which he dared to describe his new life in Christ, the struggles as well as the joys, with refreshing candor. It was not the serene, problem-free life that most Christian pastors and authors offered us. We were given encouragement to be real—honest with God, ourselves, and other people. And after all, isn't that what Jesus wants for us all?

John Westfall's book fits in that same category. He tells us in contemporary terms what it is like to be a somewhat nonconformist Christian. God loves the people who color outside of the lines as much as He loves the outwardly pietistic. He has not turned his children out with a cookie cutter. He enables each of us to be the unique persons we were meant to be. If you do not fit the traditional mold of what a Christian is supposed to look like, this book will be a great encouragement and confirmation that God is in the reality business.

Some of our false expectations about Christian behavior come from a mistranslation of the Greek *teleios* as "perfect." The common English translation is "Be perfect, even as your heavenly Father is perfect." That implies there is a particular pattern to fit, and we feel constrained to present a perfect front to the world and especially to the rest of the Christian community.

In point of fact, *teleios* means "unique" or "complete." We are commanded to be the unique, unrepeatable miracle that only we can be, just as God is the one and only Creator and Redeemer. It is a liberating truth, and one that John's book underlines with humor and clarity.

John has been my colleague and friend and beloved brother for the past eight years. I can tell you that he lives out everything that he speaks about in this book. When we first met, I assessed John as a wild and crazy kind of guy (in Steve Martin's parlance). That he is, in a wonderful and refreshing way, as well as a deeply committed, evangelical, faithful, and conscientious pastor. He has had a phenomenal ministry at University Presbyterian Church in Seattle, taking a struggling singles' department and turning it into a flourishing, vibrant ministry that has touched the lives of a thousand or more men and women, pointing them to commitment and community and outreach.

A Charlie Chaplin look-alike contest took place in Monte Carlo many years ago while Chaplin was still alive. He entered the contest and came in third. So often we do not recognize the genuine article—there are so many pretenders around. John Westfall is the genuine article, and this fresh and down-to-earth book can help you to get in touch with the real you, with God, and with all the excitement and challenge of the Christian life.

ACKNOWLEDGMENTS

It's impossible to adequately thank all of the people who contributed to the writing and publishing of this book. This was in many ways a group effort because living and writing aren't done well in a vacuum. Often the writing tasks go against the natural tendencies of "undisciplined disciples" like me. Because of this, it has taken an inordinant amount of encouragement, support, and tangible assistance for this book to see the light of day.

Bruce Larson, my pastor, mentor, and friend shaped much of my theology through his excellent books, brilliant preaching, and loving encouragement. Hazel Larson gave a precious gift of her time and expertise editing the early chapters. Marty Folsom challenged me to think in structured ways and provided the subtitles for the main sections of the book.

I have been blessed with many marvelous friends who have taught me through the laughter, tears, and fights. Special thanks to Tom Burley, Jim Garrison, Randy Rowland, Rich Hurst, Gary Winkleman, and Tim Snow.

Lonnie Hull, my editor at Harper San Francisco, has been unrelenting in her encouragement. Thank you for believing in me as well as in this book. Other members of the Harper team are Noreen Norton, Christine Anderson, and Beth Weber.

I appreciate my University Presbyterian Church family who cared for me, loved me, and gave me freedom to explore, experiment, and grow without fear of failure or success. To the single adults in my life who shared their struggles and joys, I'm especially grateful.

Behind the scenes, my parents, Frank and Laurel Westfall, have supported, encouraged, and contributed to this book with their love and zest for life.

Finally, I want to thank Jimmy Johnson who at a formative time in my life was there modeling "undisciplined discipleship." He was a person who let me know I could follow Jesus and still be a real person.

INTRODUCTION

Have you noticed that most of the devotional guides and discipleship books that have been produced through the centuries have been written by morning people? These are the folks whose body clocks prompt them to rise early in the morning to greet the day with energy and enthusiasm. They quote proverbs like "Early to bed and early to rise will make one healthy, wealthy, and wise." Unfortunately, these eager folks tend to marry someone of opposite inclinations. As a night person, I know the frustration of trying to face the day without lots of coffee. I personally don't know how anyone can function before ten o'clock in the morning.

In the church we have tended to bestow spiritual value on what may be merely a personality trait. Books on Christian maturity admonish readers to "get up an hour earlier to meet the Lord." Our hymns teach us to "come to the garden alone, while the dew is still on the roses," which is fine if you are someone who likes to get up early. But those of us who have a different personality style are left feeling guilty. We are perceived as not being spiritual enough or obedient enough, or perhaps we are just lazy in our discipleship.

There was never a time in my life when I wouldn't have considered myself a Christian. Although I had practically grown up in the church, I still never quite felt like I fit in. Although I wanted to belong, I felt one step off the pace. Whatever it was that drew a person into the inner circle of acceptance, I didn't have it. I was labeled as having a "rebellious spirit" or a "critical attitude." It wasn't that I tried to be disruptive, but what I said and did naturally seemed to go against the flow of acceptability.

Just before our wedding, the pastor took my bride-to-be aside to express his deep reservations about our impending marriage. "How can you face the rest of your life being married to someone like John?" he asked. "With so many wonderful Christian men in the church, do you really want to throw your life away with someone who dresses and looks and acts like him? He'll never amount to anything."

He was partially right, too. I didn't fit the mold that the church was looking for. I asked too many questions, I had some unpopular opinions, and I just didn't look like a Christian. But rather than give up and walk away from the church, I determined to stay and find a place where I could flourish. That decision led to seminary and the pastorate.

Nevertheless, I continued to have this lurking fear of being found out. In my first two churches, I kept thinking that if they knew what I was really like, they wouldn't want me to be their pastor. After all, I wasn't a naturally loving person, not at all like the ministers and priests portrayed in movies. I wasn't gentle and soft-spoken with a twinkle in my eye, like Bing Crosby or Dick Van Dyke. I also wasn't a forceful evangelist like Billy Graham. In fact, I got sweaty palms when I tried to share my faith with people.

It was not long before I began to believe the lie that God could not use me unless I became someone else. Who I actually was and how I naturally responded to circumstances were not acceptable for a Christian. I had to start acting differently. I began to look around for role models, Christian leaders who seemed confident, secure, effective, and well liked; those were all traits that I wanted in my life, so I tried to emulate them.

I tried to act self-assured, to avoid saying inappropriate things, to dress the way everyone else did and be what people expected me to be. I even tried getting up early for devotions (a disaster) and started dozens of prayer journals. I had the outer appearance of discipleship, but it did not seem authentic in terms of who I was. I didn't feel very free. There had to be more to being a Christian than pretending to be someone I'm not. Something had to change.

The Change

I was nervous waiting outside the door to interview for a church staff position. I wanted to present myself in the best possible light. I wanted to appear capable and creative, but if I didn't tell them of my problem in trying to fit the pastor mold, they would find our sooner or later. On the other hand, I didn't want them to think they would be buying a lemon if they hired me. Tired of pretending, I decided that I would rather not work in a church where I couldn't be myself. It was time to be real.

I began to tell my story, sharing my strengths as well as my frustrations in ministry. I told of my struggles to fit in and how I was unpredictable and impulsive in both my work and my relationships. I even confessed that I wasn't super-spiritual, that I was in fact rather undisciplined in my devotional life and, even worse, my office tended to look like a bomb just went off in it. I let them know that I was serious about my relationship with Christ, but that I was not very religious in the sense of wanting to maintain meaningless religious traditions or stilted forms of worship. Hymns have their place, but I really prefer rock and roll.

About halfway through the interview, the then senior pastor, Bruce Larson, stopped me. "It seems to me that you are one of those people who want to color outside the lines. That can be a spiritual gift—one that the church needs. It seems to me we've suffered from stereotypes in the pastoral role for too long."

Could he be right? I had been found out as someone who didn't quite fit the mold, but instead of being told to change, I was being affirmed for who I was. Those quirks of personality and temperament that I thought had to be hidden away could become spiritual gifts, to be used by God for His purposes.

The circle of affirmation had been drawn around me, and I was released to be myself in the church. Over the past eight years, I have had the exhilarating experience of watching the singles' program I direct mushroom beyond my wildest dreams.

Who knows, maybe similar exciting ministries will arise for others who find themselves coloring outside the lines. Can you picture support groups called Scribblers Anonymous, meeting to help people be themselves in this world? We all know what it's like to be in a relationship with someone who really doesn't like us the way we are. There are endless pressures, spoken and un-spoken, to change in order to please others, even other Christians.

God does not play that game with us. He embraces us as we are, complete with strengths and flaws, hopes and fears, gifts and warts. He invites us to be ourselves in relationship with Him. Many of us held back, thinking we didn't know enough or weren't good enough or spiritual enough to be a disciple of Christ. He only asks that we trust Him with every area of our lives. He already knows us better than anyone else, and He loves us regardless. Thus our relationship with Him is grounded in reality and demonstrated in personal integrity.

The call for reality is the response to a deep need for authenticity and honesty in all areas of our lives. We are growing weary of facades and cover-ups that rely on image and pretense. If our relationship with Jesus Christ is to be real, it must demonstrate itself in authentic, tangible ways.

Dictionaries tell us that "real" is something that exists in fact, authentic, genuine, permanent, and not imaginary. That is what most of us want our faith (and our lives) to become. Sadly, it is rarely an accurate description of either our lives or our faith.

A recent magazine advertisement for a credit card company featured the late John Huston, one of the greatest film directors of all time. He was discussing what separates great films from movies. Movies may have action, characters, and interesting plots, but true films of lasting value have substance, substance that elevates them beyond mere entertainment. He went on to say that he was working on "the greatest film of all, my life. Unfortunately, too often it runs like a movie."

I can relate to that. In spite of our best intentions to live lives of substance, character, and worth, we end up filling our lives with amusements, subplots, and action, all of which leaves us tired, distracted, and unfulfilled. We need a real faith for our real lives!

It is time to rediscover the radical nature of Christian discipleship. Perhaps we have been taught a style of discipleship that no longer meets the needs of today's men and women. The old form is ineffective for most of us. It simply doesn't work. Perhaps it never did work, but in deference to those spiritual pioneers who went before, we keep practicing a futile form of discipleship in our lives.

Discipleship, disciplined or not, is for everyone. It begins with the realization that God is "for" us. Whether we are strong or weak, rich or poor, self-controlled or impulsive, Jesus invites us to discover a whole new way of living as we follow Him day by day.

In these next chapters, we'll be examining styles and forms of the Christian life from a fresh perspective, one designed to encourage and enable all you would-be disciples who tend to color outside the lines.

PART I

Laying a Foundation

CHAPTER ONE

Undisciplined Discipleship

O_N a recent trip to Malaysia, while standing in line to check my bags, I watched a tour group getting ready to embark on their great adventure. Some members of the group were obvious adventurers; they traveled light with only a small duffel bag and seemed charged up and eager for the new experiences they would have on this trip. Others had a confused, frightened appearance; they looked as if this was their first big trip and they didn't know what to expect or what new danger was lurking out there in the big scary world. There were even a few bored-looking seasoned travelers who acted rather blasé about the whole process.

In discipleship, we too set out on an adventure. We, like the first disciples, are called by Jesus to follow Him on a daily walk of faith. In the same way that travelers in the airport bring their unique personalities and various amounts of baggage, we too bring to our relationship with Jesus all of who we have been and hope to become.

As we begin, it is important to check some of our baggage at the gate. We may have packed a heavy load of doubts, fears, and painful hurts from the past. We may have packed a box full of expectations, mental snapshots of what life should be, and rigid opinions that will keep us from growth and change. We'll need to set some of that aside before we embark. It will make the journey a lot easier, and we will have more fun along the way.

Don't forget that the best part of any trip is accumulating new stuff. Thus as we follow Christ, we will continually be picking up new ideas, habits, and ways to live in joy and love.

Let's begin first by looking at some old models of discipleship that may have become burdensome on our faith journey.

The Old Models

There are at least three old models of discipleship that I think make inaccurate assumptions about life in the Kingdom.

Olde Saint Model

The first model many of us revered is what I call the Olde Saint model. In this form of discipleship we become not more Christlike but more conformed to the image of what we believe a stereotyped olde saint might be. One of the marks of this style is the practice of withdrawing from everyday life, from intimate relationships, and most of all from the world.

This style of discipleship gives the appearance of spirituality, but it results in an odd combination of pride and guilt. Our feelings of insecurity and self-doubt lead us to dress up the outer person to correspond with this image of spirituality. In maintaining this image of being withdrawn and "holy," we in fact cut ourselves off from the vital living relationships we so desperately need.

The Christian walk no longer is seen as engagement with life or involvement with people. Rather, it becomes a pulling away from others and a distancing from life. Basic healthy principles are distorted for the sake of appearance. There is nothing wrong with pursuing a spartan life-style, with having quiet, solitary time with the Lord, with retreating to gain renewed vision for life and ministry. But these can become distorted in the practice of saintly withdrawal.

Rather than growing closer to God and His creation, we become aloof, less involved, and increasingly out of touch. Often we are left feeling guilty. We think we should have done more, tried harder, spent more time doing this or that. Others of us resist any notion that we are not measuring up to the invisible standards. The Olde Saint model results in alienation from community, guilt, and rebellion. We need a new model that breeds life, freedom, and spiritual vitality.

Many people have tried to live out the call to discipleship by pulling away from the world and its distractions. Under the guise of drawing near to God, they withdrew into a world of isolation and unreal spirituality. It has been going on for centuries. There were the Essenes of Jesus' time, a Jewish sect whose members holed up in desert caves and spent their time copying manuscripts. Certainly they left a valuable legacy, but their style of ministry provides a marked contrast to that of Jesus and His disciples—on the road almost every day, subject to the vagaries of weather, unexpected interruptions, uncertainty about food and lodgings. The isolated, contemplative life is a far cry from that.

Many devotional guides and much of our Christian music address this longing to escape the troubles and cares of life in order to find solace and peace in the next life. It has been wisely said that "if you don't like now, you're going to hate heaven." To be "in Christ" is to be in relationship with the Lord and His people.

As stress arises in our lives, it is tempting to think that we could be better Christians if only we were removed from the cares of everyday relationships. I've often thought that I am a much better husband and father when I'm away from my family. I am not completely comfortable when I have to stay connected to others. It seems as if relationships have within them the seeds of pain and misunderstanding. Isolating ourselves from community may free us from accountability and expectations imposed by others, but it also keeps us from knowing love and expressing it in tangible ways.

The Workbook Model

A second old model of discipleship is that of the Workbook Christian. Rather than focusing on a personal relationship with Jesus Christ, we put our trust in a set of beliefs or principles for living. This is seductive because it promises answers to questions, gives formulas for life, and defines consistent, clear-cut roles and strategies that disciples can fit themselves into. These "clone rules" come from many sources—seminars, how-to books, and even church doctrinal statements that have been separated from life-style and behavior.

A good many churches and Christian organizations tend to rely on this ineffective model of ministry. They really believe that there are basic principles of life and faith that, with practice, will unlock the secrets to spiritual maturity, as well as full and abundant living. This model for ministry offers the subtle promise that you will be spiritually mature and successful as a Christian and that all of your relationships will fall neatly into place as a result of these "right" beliefs.

I wanted that assurance desperately. I felt that I must be doing something wrong. Like many others, I had believed a lie I had been told in Sunday school—that if we come to Jesus, everything will be good and wonderful and beautiful. We sang together as children, "Jesus wants me for a sunbeam to shine for Him each day. . . . I'll be a sunbeam for Him."

Nothing would have made me happier than to be a little sunbeam for Jesus. Each week I recommitted myself to try harder and to be good and live for Him. My family would be happy, my friends would be happy, and life would be great!

But inevitably, before Sunday school was over, I was the one pushing some other kid to get out the door first. I was the one mercilessly teasing some poor little girl. On the ride home, I was the one fighting with my brother and driving my dad up the wall. No matter how hard I tried, I just couldn't be a sun-beam.

As an adult I was still haunted by the need to discover principles that would open the door to successful Christian living. I hoped Bill Gothard's "Basic Youth Conflicts" seminar would show me how to have healthy relationships, and *The Four Spiritual Laws* booklet would enable me to be a dynamic witness. I even went through *Ten Basic Steps to Christian Maturity* hoping to find the key to unlock my faith. Every once in a while I'd discover a new principle that I could apply to my life, but it never quite came together for me. I thought the problem must be within me.

With each new workshop or seminar, with every workbook and discipleship guide, I became more discouraged. These tools seemed to work for everyone else; they apparently were universal principles, so if they weren't working, I must be failing. Perhaps I didn't have enough faith, I didn't believe God enough, I hadn't studied Scripture enough, or maybe I had a secret sin that was blocking what God wanted to do in me. Therefore, I should either give up and quit because it doesn't work or get back in there and work all the harder.

In case you haven't recognized it yet, this old model is discipleship by law, a favorite of the Pharisees in Jesus' time. Simply stated, the assumption is that if these rules and steps and plans are followed rigorously, life will be full. If your life is not full, then you are to root out the principle that was violated and make the necessary changes in your life so that it will be full. This model produces rigidity not only in our beliefs but also in our relationships.

The beginning point in an honest relationship is to free ourselves from rigid roles and expectations and begin to actually share real life. That is precisely what Jesus wants to do with each of us. He doesn't want to be a little plastic statue on the dashboard. He calls out, "Get me off the dashboard and let me ride in the car with you; in fact, let me drive." But it is safer to make Him some distant religious figure. So we keep Him there on the dashboard right next to our glow-in-the-dark Elvis statue.

He says, "I don't want to be a religious icon, I want to have a relationship with you, with real conversation. Because it will be a real relationship, we will even fight at times. Sometimes you will go off in a huff to your room and not want to talk to me. That's okay, for when you come out I will still be here, waiting for you."

Just like real people. That's the way we begin to relate personally with Jesus Christ and with one another—not with rigid roles or manipulative expectations but face to face, real faith for real life.

The Military Model

The third old model is the military style of discipleship. This is marked by clear hierarchies of structure and power. In this model each person becomes the caretaker for the next person's spiritual well-being. As the discipler, you make decisions for others about their lives, child raising, marriages, jobs, and so on. It's a marvelous way to play God in someone else's life while giving up some of the responsibility for your own. Simply put, in the military model, I am discipling you, someone else is discipling me, and, typically, all three of us are under the authority of a third, more exalted, teacher and leader.

This model may be designed to promote accountability, but it actually breeds irresponsibility and dependence. If someone else is responsible for you, and you are responsible for others, then all are free from having to be responsible for themselves. There is always someone else to tell you what you should or shouldn't do; therefore, when something goes wrong it is clear whom you can blame for your misfortune.

Perhaps this is one of the reasons that books, articles, and seminars dealing with how to know God's will are so popular. If we could figure out God's will for our life, then when something goes wrong, we could blame God and use Him as a scapegoat for our misfortune. After all, if God willed our misfortune, then we are free from having to behave responsibly in our lives.

In a recent counseling session, a man blurted out, "I don't know why God told me to marry this person." I asked the man where he was when the decision was being made. Did God force him to get on his knees and propose one moonlit night when his heart was filled with passion? Oh well, if it's God's will, then it's God's fault.

Like a military hierarchy, this model provides for a chain of command. There are generals, corporals, sergeants, and privates, so that everyone knows where he or she is in clear relationship with others. Relationships become the battleground for power games and manipulation, rather than the breeding ground for the releasing creativity of the Holy Spirit.

Again, this military model has little foundation in the style of discipleship we find in the Gospels. Jesus demonstrated His authority by washing the disciples' feet. His servanthood enabled others to become strong. This is a marked contrast with the authoritarian discipler who uses personal power and position to create dependency and weakness.

A New Model

In all three of these old models, freedom is replaced with guilt, rebellion, or blind obedience. We are left once more in bondage, not knowing the freedom that is ours when we follow Jesus. Where will we find a new model of discipleship, one that does not rely on saintly withdrawal, or workbooks and techniques, or authoritarian structures, but rather sets us free to become the unique men and women God created us to be?

It is important to understand that there is only one critical issue in discipleship: our relationship with Jesus Christ. All else is peripheral. Jesus does not call us to a discipling model, or a religious commitment, or a sociopolitical cause. He calls us to a radical relationship with Him. It is radical in the sense that it is the essence of everything that we do.

Apart from this relationship with Jesus Christ, we are adrift in a sea of worthless advice, good intentions, and less than helpful guidance. Christ's challenge to today's men and women is "Trust me with your life. Get to know me, and let me know you, then we can walk through life together." We might recoil, thinking that this seems too easy, there must be a catch. But His offer is genuine. Whatever our situation or circumstance, He wants to go into it with us.

It is as if He says, "I know about the problems in your marriage, or at the office; let me go there with you. Let me be with you in the circumstance or relationship, and by the very nature of our relationship we will begin to see changes in those areas." Positive change is possible in all areas of life: in our homes, work, play, inner lives, perhaps even in the government and the church. Wouldn't it be radical if God was able to break into and make a difference in our churches? I always thought that might be the last place He'd be able to do that.

The undisciplined discipleship I'm talking about is one shorn of old models and rigid programs, but it is still costly. It begins when we allow our personal relationship with Christ to permeate every area of our lives. We begin to see ourselves as the unique persons He created us to be. All areas of our life are accessible to His healing, empowering, and directing. Most of all, we don't have to become someone else to please Him. He says, like the popular ballad of a few years back, "I love you just the way you are."

CHAPTER TWO

Unconventional Spirituality

*O*NE Sunday after church I went to a brunch buffet with my family. We happened to be seated near the salad bar, and I couldn't help noticing the different ways in which people approached the buffet.

There were the dieters who bypassed the solid foods and sampled a little salad, fruit, perhaps some cheese, while casting furtive glances at the dessert table. Some people approached the table as if they had a battle plan. They had small plates for certain items and large plates for the main dishes. They placed their food with care so that sauces and flavors didn't get mixed up. Their plates were like well laid out gardens. (These people probably never have just one sock left over in their sock drawer.)

Then there were those who approached the table with gusto and abandon. Taking their cue from the old beer commercial advice "You only go around once in life," they were out to grab it all. Their plates were piled high with every strange and exotic food. Most of the things on the bottom had merged together into a mass of indistinguishable calories. Over the top they glopped thousand island dressing, allowing it to run off the side of the plate, leaving a telltale trail back to their seats.

Our approach to the salad bar can sometimes be an indicator of how we approach life. Does our fear keep us confined to small survival rations, or do we develop plans and strategies to make the most of our circumstances? Are we grasping and consuming, trying to squeeze everything out of each moment, or are we holding back, waiting for a better offer?

We each have our own unique style in approaching life. Sometimes that style works well for us, and other times it hinders our growth. Unfortunately, even when our usual approach doesn't work, we tend to keep pursuing the destructive behavior, hoping that we will get different results. It has been said that one mark of insanity is doing the same things over and over, expecting different results. How many times in my life have I continued in old patterns, hoping things would change?

We need a fresh approach in order to move ahead in life free from the numbing traditions and behaviors that have failed to bring us the freedom or growth we desire. Conventional wisdom has not helped us to think creatively, and conventional religion has not freed us to live with abandon. We need a "Jesus style" of life, an unconventional spirituality that releases us to live passionately, with both freedom and grace.

Destination Orientation

One of the most frequently asked questions on any family trip is "Are we there yet?" In this age of instant breakfast, microwave cooking, Concorde jets, and immediate access to information via computers, we want it now!

The destination orientation seeps into every area of life. We want to have relationships, but we don't take the time to develop intimacy. We enjoy playing musical instruments but resist the daily practice necessary to develop the ability to play well. Like many authors, I like having written but dread the grind of writing. Spiritually, we long for fulfillment; we want the end result of faith more than we want to live by faith. We want to be mature, holy, wise, pure, loving, instantaneously. We are often like the person who said, "I want patience, and I want it now!"

I find it interesting that Jesus never spoke in terms of arrival or destination when He called people to be His disciples. The

Gospel accounts show Jesus inviting them to follow Him, but He doesn't tell them where they are going or when they are going to get there.

Imagine Peter trying to explain to his wife why he is leaving the family fishing business, or Matthew letting his parents know that he is giving up that great job with the tax office to follow Jesus. Can you imagine the questions this must have raised? "What do you mean, follow Jesus? Follow him where? What will you do? How will you eat? Where will you stay? Why don't you just settle down and get this foolishness out of your head?"

Following Christ today raises some of the same issues in our minds. He invites us to follow Him, but we want to know where we are going. We want Him to show us a road map and consult us on the best way to get there. But this is not faith. Faith involves letting go of our destination orientation in order to allow Christ to lead us on a daily basis. Faith is as much a journey as it is a destination.

What's Wrong with Religion?

One of the problems with religion is that it negates the need for faith. It relies on conventional spirituality with a heavy emphasis on control (both external control and self-control). At the heart of religion is our effort to win God's approval. We mistakenly think that if we could just get it right, we would be good enough to win God's love and acceptance. We would have arrived. Thus we set out to live, act, and think so that we do not jeopardize our standing with God.

Too often we think that if we can be good, perfect, strong, or quiet enough, then we will earn the love, attention, and affirmation we seek. Religion reinforces this misconception by providing standards by which our performance can be measured. Unfortunately, we never do measure up to the ideal and are left feeling undeserving of God's love or resentful that He is withholding the attention we seek.

I discovered this early in my life in an unexpected way. It was the Christmas season and my family had just returned from Africa, where we had lived the past three years, and I could hardly wait to get to the department store to see Santa Claus. He was going to be there in person, and I had heard that kids could actually climb up onto his lap and ask him questions. I was looking forward to meeting the old gentleman. I had often thought of the day when we'd meet face to face and I could thank him for what he had done and let him know what else I needed. My sister Florence and I got dressed up because they would be taking pictures of us with Santa. Flo wore a pretty dress, and I was in my best short-sleeved white shirt with clip-on bow tie, as off we went.

After what seemed an eternity of waiting in line, it was time. We each sat on one of Santa's knees, and he asked Flo what she wanted for Christmas, then gave her a candy cane. It was my turn. He turned to me and with those penetrating eyes that could bore holes through little children's hearts he asked, "Well, Johnny, have you been a good boy this year?"

I was found out. He surely knew that I had not been good at all, that I had teased my sister and not cleaned up my room. He knew me, and there was no place to hide. So as tears began to trickle down my cheeks, the fateful picture was snapped—a memento of my first visit with Santa.

Somehow we have mistakenly confused God with Santa. Think of the kinds of songs we sing at Christmas time: "He knows when you've been naughty, he knows when you've been nice," "Better watch out. . . . Santa Claus is coming to town." The performance trips we lay on children are amazing. Is it any wonder that when we are faced with an increasing inability to be good enough, we stop believing anymore?

But God is not Santa Claus. He is not a seasonal myth created to get children to behave. He came not in wrath but in love, knowing full well that we can never be perfect enough to demand His love and attention. While we may fear being exposed for who we are, He is not surprised by our inability to be perfect. In fact, He offers His own resources to enable us to live in the freedom and power of His love.

Jesus overturns the tables of religion, just as He did centuries ago. He is the evidence of God's unmerited love. In Him God has said, "I love you regardless." No longer do we strive to earn His love or gain His attention. We are loved by God, and we are known for who we are. Because of this we are free to follow Christ in an adventure of faith where we no longer control the outcome of our lives, but we learn a new way of relating and living.

Living from the Inside Out

It is impossible to live the Christian life without a relationship with Christ. Yet how is that relationship demonstrated in tangible ways? The answer to this question lies at the root of discipleship. Paul, writing to the early believers, said, "It is no longer I who lives, but it is Christ who lives in me" (Gal. 2:20 TEV). If this is true, then our goal as disciples is not to try hard to act like Christians but rather to remove anything in our lives that keeps the living Christ from expressing Himself through us.

While our natural tendency may be to present ourselves in the best light, to work hard doing the right things, and to try to be more loving, gracious, and so forth, discipleship requires us to get out of the way so that Christ may live through us. This discipleship is radical in that the focus ceases to be on us and our feeble (or heroic) attempts to better ourselves. Rather, the focus is on Christ and His transforming power.

Unfortunately, much of the church's message has traditionally focused on bringing about external changes in people rather than the inner transformation of authentic discipleship. Perhaps this is because it is easier to measure the outer actions. We can keep score and monitor one another's spiritual development by paying attention to the external behaviors. This isn't new. In fact, the Old Testament writer observed, "Man looks on the outward appearance, but the Lord looks on the heart" (I Sam. 16:7 RSV).

My family took a vacation to the beautiful country of Ireland several years ago. In the town of Waterford is the famous factory manufacturing crystal that is reputed to be the finest in the world. Near the factory tourists may visit a number of outlet stores that sell at reduced prices pieces of crystal that have been designated "seconds." To the untrained eye these glasses and vases looked perfect. The shopkeepers are quick to point out that only the clearest glass can bear the Waterford name. Pieces with bubbles, cloudiness, or flaws, or that are not clear all the way through, are said to lack purity.

It was helpful for me to realize that the word "purity" in the New Testament does not mean doing the right things or being good. It means clarity, being without blemish, clear all the way through. Impurity is the cloudiness that comes from pretending to be what we are not.

When we lie to ourselves and others, when we cover up and pretend to be what we are not, when we live in denial and refuse to acknowledge our own sin, we are not pure. Discipleship is most of all demonstrated in a transparent purity in which we become the same on the outside as we are on the inside.

Through the discipleship process God is enabling men and women to live pure lives, clear all the way through. And one way of maintaining this kind of purity, or integrity, is by being vulnerable with a few people in your life.

Vulnerability

Personally, I'm not very comfortable with this word. It goes against many of my natural tendencies. I don't particularly like sharing, and I don't instinctively like others getting too close to me. But God didn't ask my opinion, and I'm not the one making up the rules in this relationship.

Since our standing with God is based on our relationship with Him and not on our beliefs or behaviors, it is important to understand what nurtures intimate relationships and what hinders them. It is also important to begin to live out in all areas of life the traits of our inner relationship with Christ.

Lloyd Ogilvie has said that "vulnerability involves giving to others the weapons that can hurt us." This goes against our tendency toward self-protection. We all have sensitive areas in our lives that we don't want others to know. Many of us have secrets that can harm us if they become known. To protect ourselves, we conceal our failures, weaknesses, and frustrations, hoping that if they remain buried for a long enough time, they will simply go away.

But that is not usually what happens. Rather than diminishing, our secrets begin to consume us. Like the guilty man in Edgar Allan Poe's "The Telltale Heart," we are haunted by those things that we hide away. On the other hand, we become released from those things in our life that we confess. When we share a problem, a personal struggle, or a failure from the past, it looses its grip on us, and its power over us is lessened.

This is why confession is crucial in the lives of Christian disciples. It is an act of vulnerability that sets us free to move forward in our relationship with God and other people. The biblical mandate is to "confess your sins one to another," (James 5:16 TEV) and to conceal your strengths: "When you pray go into your room" (Matt. 6:6 NIV). That is a radical departure from what is generally practiced in our society. We are inundated with well-meaning advice to conceal our weaknesses or flaws and to accentuate our strengths. Our interest in self-esteem, positive thinking, attitude adjustment, or whatever, encourages today's men and women to present themselves in the best way possible.

As a result, we have cultivated a generation of people who posture and pose for one another, striving to present a good image while at the same time being consumed in obsessive-compulsive behavior. Our secrets control us, and our strengths lose their effectiveness, because we have practiced a life-style that is the polar opposite of what Christ intended for His disciples.

We may not like being vulnerable, but the alternative is a life of quiet desperation, in which we are neither known nor loved for who we are. If we only present the good side, we can never know that someone has seen us at our worst and still chooses to love us.

Intimacy in relationships begins when we give the gift of our true self, complete with strengths and flaws, to another person. We in effect say, "Knowing me this way, you have the power to hurt me, but I love you enough to let you know me."

At the church I serve, one of my least favorite parts of the worship service is the Prayer of Confession. In most churches the pastor can read a prepared confession filled with vague generalities about our corporate failure to be all that we can be. But a few years ago at a staff meeting, it was decided that whoever had that assignment in the worship service should just confess his or her own sin from the previous week. That seemed more authentic and in turn would model genuine confession for the congregation.

One particular Sunday, I was assigned that prayer in the service. It had been a terrible week for me, one in which family tensions had dominated. I wasn't feeling very spiritual, and I was not acting very loving toward my wife, my son, or God. So I did the sensible thing and wrote out a vague, generic, religious-sounding confession to be read in the service.

Sitting in front of the congregation that morning, I felt far from the people, far from my family, far from God, and I was pouting because I felt sorry for myself. My mind was anywhere but on worship as I got up to read my confession. Just then my brain shorted out and I lost my presence of mind, and instead of reading the written prayer I said, "Lord, You know that this has been a terrible week. I have been a jerk at home, and I was so unloving that I put my fist through the bedroom wall while fighting with my wife. I need Your forgiveness. Amen." I sat down.

You could have heard a pin drop in the sanctuary. Several things happened that morning. Immediately following the service, three contractors offered their services to replaster my bedroom wall. But more importantly, I was suddenly freed to worship in a fresh way. There were no secrets to hold inside.

Everyone knew now that I was not a loving, patient saint of a husband and father. I was able to experience the healing that comes when we allow ourselves to be the recipients of grace. (I decided to leave the hole in the wall as a tangible reminder of my struggle to be loving and my continuing desire to control my temper.)

Unconventional spirituality is grounded in an authentic relationship with Jesus Christ. It isn't measured by our performance, and it isn't overly concerned with a destination. What does matter is that we begin to live from the inside out, being women and men who dare to live transparently in a world that knows only superficial imaging. It is not an easy way to live, but it is the only way to know the freedom that Christ intends for His disciples.

CHAPTER THREE

Unreal Expectations

EVER since the very first Christmas, there have been people who have felt let down. Following my first disappointing encounter with Santa, in which I remembered that I had not been a good boy, I determined to set things right.

Beginning New Year's Day of the next year, I made up my mind that I would be good. I worked hard and made every effort toward goodness. Not being completely greedy, I figured Santa could give most of his gifts to the more needy children. All that I needed to make my life complete . . . was a pair of cowboy chaps. I already had the boots, hat, and vest. I even had a Roy Rogers insignia headboard over my bed. I had a Roy Rogers pistol and a Texas John Slaughter souvenir holster. (Slaughter was left-handed like me and drew his guns crosswise in the movies.) I had everything necessary to be a cowboy except the chaps.

When the Christmas J. C. Penney catalog arrived, instead of sitting down and writing a long list of toys, I held back. This showed an amazing degree of restraint. I wrote a simple note: "Dear Santa, It was good to see you last year [that was a lie]. I'm looking forward to seeing you again this year when you come to the Whittier Quad [that was a lie as well]. Santa, you can give all those gifts away to the poor kids, because all I want is a pair of chaps. Love Johnny."

I licked the stamp and sent it off to the North Pole. A few weeks later, I heard the news that Santa would be at the shopping center. I wasn't about to miss my chance. I was ready, and this time I didn't take Florence along. After waiting patiently in line, it was finally my turn. I climbed right up onto his lap, and when he asked me, "Have you been a good boy this year?" I blurted out, "I sure have, and you know it!"

He then asked me, "What do you want for Christmas?" I suspected that this was just part of his game, because he certainly had received my letter by now. Looking at him with great confidence, I said, "Like I mentioned in the letter, Santa, I don't want anything, except those cowboy chaps." As he gave me a candy cane, he looked at me with those knowing eyes and flashed a confidential wink, as if to say, "Don't worry, I've got you covered."

I was fine. On Christmas Eve my brothers and sister were nervous, but not me. I knew that I had gotten through to Santa, and there was nothing for me to worry about. While I slept, I dreamt that I was riding the range with my new cowboy chaps.

The next morning everyone was running around the house, saying, "Santa came, Santa came." Well, I knew that Santa had come, so I sauntered into the living room cool and slow and sat down on the sofa. Glancing around, I saw my package under the tree, and I didn't run for it. Why should I—this was a moment to savor. Sitting back, I watched the other kids ripping at their presents, until my dad finally said, "Johnny, are you going to open your present?"

I walked over and picked up my package. Kneeling beside it, I tore off the wrapping paper, then opened the box. Reaching down past the tissue paper, my heart beat with excitement, until . . . "Wait a minute, this isn't soft, like chaps. This is hard and cold, like metal." I pulled out a truck—a Tonka dumptruck!

Something was terribly wrong. Santa hadn't gotten the message, or perhaps had been confused and mixed up the presents. Somewhere in the universe, my chaps had been delivered to the wrong child. As I sat by the tree, crying, I was confronted with the disappointment of Christmas.

Faith Is Difficult

There is something inherently difficult about putting our faith in Jesus Christ. It has to do with our expectations, hopes, and dreams, and the way that our deepest longings are either met or left unfulfilled. Faith requires us to set aside our inappropriate expectations and take hold of reality.

The world that Jesus entered wasn't very different from our own. People had hopes and dreams, plans and schemes. Many of them were waiting for someone who would come along and make their lives better.

Religiously and politically, an unmet longing hung in the air. People desired to be free, prosperous, and fulfilled. In that way they weren't very different from people today. There was a messianic hope and fervor that was based on the belief that someday God would send a deliverer who would bring freedom and healing.

Imagine people sitting around on street corners, talking about the deliverer. "When the Messiah comes, he will be a strong, charismatic leader." "If David was handsome, the Messiah will be radiant." "He will have the kind of personality that surely will draw rich and powerful people to his side. Of course, he will also be generous, so that some of that vast wealth will be spread to all of us."

Some people pictured the Messiah as a political figure. Like a benevolent dictator in a banana republic, he would take care of problems and make their lives secure. He would be strong, yet kind and gentle. What a great Messiah that would be. He would make everyone feel safe and secure while he provided for their needs. If necessary, he might rise up like a great warrior, a Jerusalem Rambo who would charge out fighting battles and destroying enemies, so that the people in turn could feel more powerful. Is it any wonder that people seemed disappointed with Jesus? Many of their hopes were left unfulfilled when God entered their world.

John the Baptist, Jesus' cousin, was confused. He was one of those people who make eccentricity almost an art form. He might have related to Salvador Dali's observation, "The only difference between me and a madman is that I'm not mad." John was a prophet who confronted others, disciplined himself, wore odd clothes, and ate strange food. He went around telling everyone who would listen that the Messiah was coming. John's message was fear inducing. He emphasized that God was angry, so people had better get their lives in order. He preached about a Messiah who would baptize with fire. John said that the Messiah would bring judgment and punishment to the disobedient.

In Matthew 3 John proclaims, "The axe is already at the root of the trees, and he will cut down all the branches and throw them on the eternal fire where they will be consumed for eternity, for every tree that doesn't produce good fruit."

Is it any wonder, then, that John the Baptist, sitting in prison during the final days of his life, was confused when he heard the reports of what Jesus was doing. John had announced that Jesus was the one they had waited for. He began to wonder what was happening. Where was the fire? Where was the judgment? Where was the axe laid to the root of the tree?

Sitting in prison, he might have wondered, "How could I have been so wrong? How could I have missed what God was saying? Is Jesus the one, or should we look for someone else?" John sent his disciples to find out what was going on. His expectations kept him from trusting in Jesus.

Inadequate Expectations

What do we expect from God? We bring many expectations to our relationship with Christ. These expectations can set us up to be disappointed when we meet Christ. Sometimes what we are looking for will lead us to close our hearts and balk at His call to follow Him by faith. Letting go of our preconceived ideas and accepting Christ on His terms is a first step in discovering an unassailable faith.

One of our expectations is that God will send us a caped crusader. We want our Messiah to be someone who will take up our particular cause. We want Him to show the world that we are right. Jesus has been portrayed in many different ways according to people's desire for Him to vindicate their hopes. Back in the sixties there was a book, *Jesus the Revolutionary*, that portrayed Jesus as the leader of an underground movement. Peace activists portray Jesus as a pacifist. (I can almost picture Him walking around a cocktail party wearing a turtleneck sweater with a peace medallion.)

People who advocate a strong military, show Christ as a great warrior, leading the mighty army of faith against the forces of evil. Imagine the troops singing, "Onward Christian Soldiers" while Jesus leads them to victory. Others might see Jesus as a missionary Messiah wearing a pith helmet and carrying a machete.

There is also Jesus in a charcoal gray suit and power tie heading up the elevator of the office tower, the "business Jesus" of Main Street, helping us with our investment portfolios. Imagine Jesus with a boom box heading into the urban scene to be an inner city Lord. We think we can use Christ for our particular causes or special interests. Then we get offended when we meet the real Jesus.

Another expectation is for the Messiah to be our butler in waiting. We see Him as a valet or errand boy who stands on the periphery of our lives until we ring. At our bidding, He comes, serving us, catering to our needs; then He quietly adjourns to the sidelines where He patiently waits for our next call.

Some people want a Savior who will act like an obedient child, preferably one who is seen and not heard. We bring Him out at holidays or special occasions to meet and greet our friends, then we ask Him to please disappear while we talk about adult things. This happens when we think that the Christian faith is for children. Presuming that the Bible is a collection of colorful stories to amuse and instruct kids, we become unable to develop a real faith that addresses our real lives. It's as if we go along functioning with a fifth grade Sunday school education, wondering why our faith doesn't seem to make a difference in our world. It is essential to realize that the Bible was written by adults for adults. Jesus will not be our childish playmate who is seen but not heard.

Another expectation is that the Lord will be our sugar daddy. He will be someone who comes to us when we feel lonely or discouraged. He comforts us when life isn't working out the way we had hoped it would. As our sugar daddy, He brings lots of presents, good times, and warm, fuzzy feelings. We feel great when Jesus comes to visit, but when He leaves, we feel lonely again. We like being with Him because we feel good and so well cared for when He is in our life.

It has been said that the greatest disappointment in life is to not get what you want, and the second is to get what you want. The difficulty of faith does not exist because we expect too much from God and He can't live up to our expectations. Our problem is that we expect too little, and we won't receive what He has to give.

George MacDonald in his anthology writes, "Man finds it hard to get what he wants, because he does not want the best. God finds it hard to give, because He would give the best, but man will not take it."

All of these expectations fall short because they are limited by our desire to shape and control the world. By establishing expectations for Christ, we miss the freedom that comes from openly receiving God's free gift of abundant life.

We are becoming masters at living so that there will be no surprises, so that we remain in control. We search for clues that will alert us to what is coming. We substitute orderliness for passion and predictability for freedom.

When I first asked Eileen to go on a date with me, she asked, "Where are we going?" "How 'bout dinner and a movie?" I responded. Then she interrogated me about the choice of restaurant and which movie I wanted to see.

"Why don't you let me surprise you?" I asked. Finally she admitted, "I don't like surprises, because I don't trust you. Your surprise will probably not be a good one."

We can be that way with God. We don't want to be surprised because deep down we don't trust Him. We don't believe that His surprises will be good. We'd rather keep things predictable and controlled.

I once received a strange Christmas card from a friend. It showed Santa Claus dressed up in a big red Easter Bunny suit, carrying an Easter basket filled with candy canes. The card said, "Great men are never predictable."

Jesus Christ will never be predictable. Yet our expectations of Him, whether as a caped crusader or errand boy, an obedient child or a sugar daddy, are all attempts to use Him for our purposes. We attempt to make Him small enough to be controlled so that our world will be safe and our perspectives will remain intact. This is why Jesus says to John's followers, "Blessed is he who takes no offense at me" (Matt. 11:6 RSV).

The good news is that no matter how hard we strive to limit the power of God in our lives, or bind up the Holy Spirit through our attitudes and expectations, or shrink our worldview, or narrow our vision, He is still Lord.

Jesus is Lord of our circumstances, attitudes, and prejudices. He is Lord of our visions, hopes, fears, relationships, and careers. He is Lord of our families, finances, bedrooms, and kitchens. He is Lord of our past, present, and future.

He is not limited by our abilities and resources. Nor is he intimidated by our circumstances, fears, or insecurities. He will lead us according to His purposes when we allow Him to be involved in our whole life.

The Seattle Mariners, when owned by George Argyros, created a surprising controversy by firing God. It seems that God was being blamed for their losing seasons. The owner thought that if he could just get God out of the locker room, the team might win more games. He thought there were too many Christians on the team, and that prayer and Bible study were causing them to lose ball games.

A local reporter interviewed Steve Largent, who was playing football for the Seattle Seahawks, and asked him what he thought of the move to get God out of the locker room. He responded by saying, "It makes sense to me for them to get rid of God. The Mariners always trade away their best players. If one part of the team is producing, they try to get rid of him."

To my dismay, the director of the Council of Churches agreed with the Mariners' position. "If those players want to meet God, they can go to church like everyone else," he said. "They shouldn't take God into the locker room anymore than you would expect a banker to take his faith into the bank when he goes to work."

Our faith becomes negotiable precisely at the point where we discover what it means to follow Christ in all of life. He wants to be with us where we live, work, and play.

The Old Testament prophet describing the Messiah said, ". . . as one from whom they hide their faces he was despised, and we esteemed him not" (Is. 53:3 RSV). Today we still find excuses to turn away from the face of Christ. Perhaps we hide from Him because He isn't what we expected. We may hide because of our guilt and shame. Some may turn away out of disinterest or preoccupation. Still others may turn aside, pursuing lesser gods.

It is our choice. We can settle for second best, rather than looking into the face of the One who can make a difference. We can work hard to squeeze Jesus into our image of what we think He ought to be. Or we can accept Him by faith, opening up all of our lives to His care.

"I saw the Lord," Dallas Holm sang.

> He was high and lifted up,
> and rightfully adored.
> I saw the Lord,
> and He saw me.

As you turn toward Jesus Christ and look into His face, you discover that He is already looking at you. When you reach out to Him, He is already taking hold of you. As you open the hidden parts of your life that you would prefer remain secret, He says, "I already knew that and I love you anyway."

Turning to Him our faith becomes authentically strong, and we become a new creation. The old has passed away, and all things are made new. Jesus said, "Go and tell them what you have seen and heard. Happy will be the person who is not offended by me."

CHAPTER FOUR

Unstoppable Living

*E*VERYONE has a next step. Some of those next steps, or changes, are imposed from the outside, while at other times pressures from within force us to move forward. Change can bring with it large amounts of stress and frustration. Stress comes when we seek to move forward in growth and change but feel paralyzed, blocked, or held back.

Contrary to what others may tell you, life isn't one continuous procession of happiness and good times. There are tough times, when nothing seems to work out, when people you love disappoint you, when pain reminds you every day that it's not going away.

I had the privilege of interviewing Dr. Norman Vincent Peale and his wife, Ruth, for my "Everyday People" radio program. Knowing that his book *The Power of Positive Thinking* had helped millions of people, I was looking forward to discussing it with him.

I began the interview by asking Ruth if her husband was really positive all the time, or did he struggle like many of us with insecurity, discouragement, and fear. She smiled and said, "He's always had to deal with those things; that's why I encouraged him to write the book, because I thought it would help him with some of these negative feelings."

Norman then responded, "Like others, I've struggled with those traits, but I believe what I wrote, and I practice it in my own life. Most of all, I have learned that through my relationship with Jesus Christ, I have the power to live beyond myself."

Isn't this the key to unstoppable living? To allow Jesus Christ to live in us and enable us to live beyond ourselves. It is not merely trying harder to accomplish more on our own strength. Neither is it giving up and becoming content with whatever comes our way. Rather, it is moving forward in life in spite of the obstacles, failures, and fears that we inevitably experience.

Life in the Pits

Do you ever feel stuck? Bogged down? Like you're unable to move forward? It can be terribly frustrating wanting to move ahead but finding yourself unable to get unstuck. It's a little like the recurring dream I had as a child, in which I was being chased by a horrible monster, but the harder I tried to run, the more I moved in slow motion. I just couldn't get myself going.

When we are in the pits, inevitably others will come along and offer advice and wisdom for our situation. Some will say, "There are no pits." They advise us to think positively and show a positive mental attitude, and we will do just fine. Remember those old show tunes that taught us how to deal with adversity by putting on a happy face, or using the true antidote for fear—whistling a happy tune. Imagine walking through a dark alley at night and being confronted by muggers. Just whistle a happy tune—that ought to frighten them off!

Some people are what I call Helium Christians. They act like they are floating a foot off the ground. They don't want to hear about hard times; they just want to stay "spiritual" and happy and praise the Lord. When you try to share a problem with them, you can sense their discomfort. They like to remind you that you just need more faith, then everything will be wonderful for you too. Of course, like helium balloons, they are filled with gas, and eventually they will come down from that spiritual high.

In contrast to the Helium Christians there are the dreaded Pit Dwellers, those morose folks who believe in the power of negative thinking and have chosen to live their lives in the gloom and doom of life's pits. They tend to believe that all life is a pit, and we will never get out. Why should we struggle when there will only be new problems down the road? This defeatist attitude bids them to give up because there is no hope. We see that mind-set reflected in the bumper stickers some cynics have put on their cars: "Life is hard, then you die."

Pit Dwellers tend to feel secure as long as bad things are happening, and they usually have a group of grumbling buddies to support them in their depressed condition. Unfortunately, they too often miss out on the great things God wants to do in them and through them in our world.

Neither of these viewpoints is rooted in reality. We need a fresh perspective in order to unlock the secret for unstoppable living. We need a perspective that is realistic, not just about the pain in life but also about the resources God provides to move beyond the pain. John Fischer has summed up the tension we experience in his reminder "Life is hard, but God is good."

Having lived a few years in the jungles of Africa, I guess it was natural that I would be drawn to Tarzan movies on Saturday afternoons. Tarzan was a hero for me as he swung through the trees solving problems and battling wrongs.

Those movies invariably include a scene in which a villain veers off the trail and wanders into the clearing where there is a pit of quicksand. Inevitably, he calls for help, but no one is able to rescue him. The more he thrashes and struggles to free himself from the terrible ooze, the deeper into the pit he sinks, until all that is left is a pith helmet floating on the surface of the swamp.

Imagine the impact such scenes had on me. I began to carry a long stick when I went out to play . . . in Whittier, California. I was diligent in my search for dangerous places in the backyard where quicksand might be lurking. It was not until a few years later that I learned how the suction of quicksand increases when you struggle to get free. To keep from sinking, you need only to resist the natural urge to struggle and instead spread your arms wide, tilt back your head, and float quietly on the surface. You will not sink as you wait to be rescued.

But try convincing a little kid that she shouldn't fight to get out of quicksand. Try convincing an adult that he need not struggle when he finds himself in the pits of life. It goes against our natural tendencies. When we are in desperate situations, when relationships are crumbling, our jobs are going down the drain, our finances are in disarray, or our marriages seem dull and listless, our natural urge is to struggle. We will try, do, or promise anything just to make something happen. But the more we kick out against the darkness, the deeper into the pit we sink.

King David must have felt some of this frustration when he wrote in Psalm 40,

> I waited for the Lord,
> he listened and heard my cry
> and pulled me up out of the miry bog.
> He put me on a firm rock
> and made my steps secure.

He seemed to have found an answer in waiting for the Lord to make a difference in his situation.

It's About Time

Waiting is never easy. Forced to wait in difficult times, a doubting voice inside us says, "You've waited too long, there is no hope, nothing will happen, God has forgotten you." Don't believe it!

Some of us have to wait longer than others. Some of us are better at waiting than others. Some of us cause others to wait. In my marriage Eileen was the "waiter" while I was the "waitee." I was always late, and it drove her crazy. I didn't think of myself as late so much as chronologically creative. I found other uses for time, and I usually wasn't where I said I'd be when I said I'd be there. For me it seemed as if time stood still while I fit more activities into my schedule.

Part of the problem is that we bring into our relationships perceptions about time that we assume the other person understands. Then we wonder what's wrong when people don't see things the way we do. In the first years of my marriage, we had an ongoing fight over time perceptions. Each day I'd call home in the early afternoon, and Eileen would ask what time I was coming home. I'd say that I would be home for dinner. When I arrived at home at around 7:00 P.M. she would be angry, and the dinner would usually be burned, cold, or thrown away. At this point we would predictably have an argument in which she would accuse me of being thoughtless and insensitive and I in turn would accuse her of being unreasonable and demanding.

After years of following this little marital ritual, we finally had a breakthrough. I arrived home at my usual time, and instead of arguing with me, Eileen simply asked, "What time do you think we eat dinner?"

"We eat at 7:30, we have always eaten at 7:30. My family always ate at 7:30, and I expect I will always eat at that time," I replied.

"Wrong!" She said. "We always eat at 5:30. We have always eaten at 5:30, my family always ate at 5:30, and we are not about to change that dinner hour!"

Suddenly we realized that we were both right. We had expectations about time that we had not bothered to share with each other, and those expectations had been the basis for our feelings of frustration and misunderstanding for a long time.

The same miscommunication can take place in our relationship with God. We cry out, "Where were You when I needed You? I've been waiting—don't You care, don't You love me?"

God in turn says, "Of course I love you, but my timing and your expectations about my timing are not always the same. I do love you and will be there for you."

Faith involves trusting not only that God will be there for us but also trusting His timing in our lives. A friend gave my wife and me a gift of a beautiful handpainted clock with the words "God's Timing Is Perfect" around the face. It is a daily reminder that God may not act according to our expectations or according to our schedule, but we can still trust that His timing is perfect.

When we find ourselves in the pits, it is easy to think that no one is listening, or that no one cares, or that our prayers are ignored or unheeded by God. We may intellectually realize that is not true, but the feelings remain. Most of us know what it feels like when no one is listening to us. Have you ever poured out your heart to someone, only to realize she has tuned you out or is preoccupied with her own problems, needs, or concerns? You felt devalued, a nonperson.

It is important during difficult times to remember that we have God's undivided attention. Picture the Lord, Creator of the universe, loving Father, personally committed to you. He is tuned in to hear your cares, worries, hopes, and dreams. You fill His heart. There is no one more important to God right now than you. Let Him know the longings of your heart, for He is listening to you.

A Question of Trust

In whom will you trust? There are lots of slimy pits all around us that claim to be firm ground on which we can stand. But when we step out trusting in these lesser gods, they cannot hold our weight, and we find ourselves slipping into a pit.

So many things—people, money, sex, career, religion, patriotism, possessions, families—seem at first like solid ground. They all cry out, "Stand on me! I'll make you sure, I'll make you steady, I'll give you what you want or need. Stand on me!" Initially they may appear solid, but they don't support us over the long haul.

If we put our trust in anything or anyone but Jesus Christ, we are setting ourselves up for disappointment. These things to which we cling only hold us back and keep us unable to experience the unstoppable power of Christ.

Unfortunately, many of us have had negative experiences in our lives that have caused us to pull away from trusting relationships. Perhaps early experiences undermined our ability to lean on God, or to feel secure in our relationship with Him. That insecurity can lead us to wonder where we stand with God from one moment to the next.

I remember sitting in a chapel service at my Baptist elementary school, listening to the principal give a devotional. At the end of his talk, he asked those who wanted to become Christians to raise their hands. I was already a Christian, so I kept my hand down. Then he asked if we wanted to "be sure that we were sure that we were saved," and that got me. I was pretty sure, but I wasn't sure that I was sure, so I raised my hand and accepted Jesus into my life one more time, just to be safe.

Later in junior high, whenever guest preachers or evangelists spoke at the evening service, they inevitably asked if anyone wanted to be sure they were sure of their standing with God. I would feel that old insecurity creeping back, and down the aisle I would go once again to get it right. In the following few years I must have accepted Christ as my Savior at least fifty times. I was looking for a confident assurance of where I was with God, but all those commitments left me even more insecure about my relationship with Him.

Finally, in college I gave up. I told God that I was tired of the insecurity of not knowing whether He was in my life or not, and I was tired of feeling guilty every time a guest speaker visited the church. "God, either you be in my life, or get out and let me go my own way," was my ultimatum.

It was as if He said, "Whew, why did you take so long? I was with you back at the beginning; why don't you let go of your insecurity and start trusting me?" You see, we can't enjoy driving a car if we are continually sitting in the garage starting and restarting the engine. God wants us to trust Him and move out into life so we can see how reliable and powerful He is for every situation in which we find ourselves.

When we find ourselves blocked in life, when we find ourselves in the pits, when we feel that we can't go on by our own strength, the Lord says, "Let me be your rock, the solid foundation to make you solid. I will give you my power so that you will be able to live beyond your own resources and abilities."

On my son Damian's ninth birthday we went to see the premiere of the movie *Labyrinth*. It's not exactly a life-changing motion picture, but Damian was so excited that he threw up in the planter box outside the theater just waiting in line to go in.

The story featured a young girl on a quest to rescue her baby brother from the evil gnome king. Along the way she encounters frightening obstacles to block her way, and she also acquires a number of fellow travelers to share her journey. The worst obstacle is the dreaded Bog of Eternal Stench—a slimy lake of ooze that reeks foully and that carries a terrible curse: If you fall or step into the bog, the smell will stay on you for eternity. A pretty frightening thought for a nine-year-old and his parents.

As might be expected, the travelers, in trying to cross the Bog of Eternal Stench, get stuck in the middle of the lake, unable to reach the other side, and the ground on which they are standing begins to sink into the bog. It looks as if there is no hope, nowhere to turn, and no one to help. They are trapped with no way to escape their terrible smelly fate.

Just then one of the creatures, a large hairy monster, throws back his head and cries out in a loud wail. Suddenly, with much bubbling and churning from the depths of the oozing bog, a rock arises onto which the whole company can step to reach the safety of solid ground.

Resting on the other side, the little girl turns to her monster companion and asks why the rock came out of the water to help them at just the right moment. The hairy creature answers with simple monster logic, "Rock . . . my friend."

It's a line that translates into good theology. For those of us who would follow Jesus Christ, there are times when our way is blocked, our dreams are shattered, our strength is gone. But there is always hope because Jesus is the Rock, and He will be there for us when we need Him most. When we least expect it,

He will bring us through difficulties and into victory, for no better reason than because He loves us. Temporary setbacks and apparent defeat are not the end of the story, for the Rock is our friend.

PART II

Recoloring Old Lines

CHAPTER FIVE

Unavoidable World

I believe that many families are pathological, and that if you happen to be from one of them it will eventually get to you. The unavoidable circumstance is life in the family. We have families that we grew up in, families that we marry into, families that we align ourselves with, and perhaps the most dysfunctional of all, the church family.

Family relationships can be complex and treacherous waters through which we navigate. They are equally a source of great joy and affirmation and a focus of much pain and disappointment. How we respond to the challenges of negotiating the difficult straits of family life can be a test of our faith. There is perhaps no more difficult arena in which to practice discipleship than with the persons who know us best.

Have you ever had the sense that perhaps you were born into the wrong family? In fourth grade my best friend was Bobby Dodder. I thought he had the greatest family in the world. His mom looked (to me) like Donna Reed. His little sister showed appropriate respect to those of us who were older and wiser. His dad even had a stamp collection, just like me. In fact, his dad offered to trade stamps with me. I would give him the sheets of uncanceled African stamps we brought home from Cameroon, and he would give me lots of canceled American stamps in exchange! I loved Bobby's family.

I wanted to play in their yard, eat at their table, hang out at their house whenever I could. Bobby, on the other hand, always wanted to be over at my house, which didn't make any sense to me. He loved hanging out with the Westfalls—playing in our yard, eating at our table. He even thought that my little sister was great to hang around with.

One characteristic of life in the unavoidable world is that we don't get to choose our families. God did not ask me which family I wanted to be born into. (I think I could have helped Him in the selection process, but maybe He didn't need my help.) Likewise, we don't choose our fellow travelers in the journey of faith.

Imagine one of the first disciples, Peter, excitedly climbing out of his fishing boat and trotting off to follow Christ. We can imagine that before too long he might look around uncomfortably and ask Jesus what these other people were doing with them, and when would those others be returning home. "Lord, I understand why You bid me to be a disciple. After all, You no doubt recognized my personal strength, natural wit, and charm, and, of course, my leadership potential. But Master, look at the losers who are tagging along with us; can't You get rid of them?"

The first disciples, like us, soon realized that no one follows Jesus alone. When we say yes to Him, we are immediately thrust into a family not of our choosing: the family of God. These relationships are unavoidable. We must learn to live in grace and peace with those who are not like us.

Life in the unavoidable world is filled with frustrations and circumstances beyond our control. How we handle these things will determine the quality of our lives and our own characters. Faced with difficult situations, we are tempted to become either irresponsible or overresponsible.

Irresponsible

One response to the unavoidable family world is to retreat and hide ourselves from painful situations. Recently I went home from the office and turned off the telephone, turned up the electric blanket to high, and went into deep hibernation. I didn't want to see anyone, talk to anyone, help anyone, or care for anyone. I was retreating from life. Fortunately it only lasted about twelve hours, and I had to go out and face the world again. Some of us hide out from others because of our fear that we will not have what it takes to survive, let alone succeed.

It is possible to spend a lifetime retreating from one thing or another. Our personal lives can become carefully constructed emotional compounds designed to make the world go away. It is easy to become distrustful and overly self-protective. People are seen as unwanted interruptions in our neatly scheduled day. Finishing reports takes precedent over playing with our children or relating to our spouse. Little by little, we begin to isolate ourselves from those we love, until the barriers seem too big to cross.

I'm not knocking our need for quiet time, or moments of reflection, or even good old escapism. The problem is in wanting to stay there. We can hide out by filling our lives with work, or with the help of a bottle of alcohol or pills. We can hide behind the facade of our marriage or our singleness. Even the church can become a snug harbor that shields us from real life.

Short-term relationships can become a hiding place from the frustration of the unavoidable world. I enjoy traveling to other places to speak at retreats and conferences because that adds an element of excitement and freshness to my job as a pastor. The downside is that it is easy to develop pseudointimacy with people who will only know me for two or three days. As a speaker, I can control how I am perceived. I can present myself as charming, witty, fun, spiritual, entertaining, and even slightly dangerous for a relatively short period of time. In that controlled environment, I can appear as a fascinating, utterly loveable person. Besides, anyone who travels more than a hundred miles and shows slides is considered an expert, thus a certain amount of respect is bestowed on one automatically.

When I return home, I am met by a family that is fairly unimpressed by my charm and wisdom, by staff colleagues who are unmoved by my wit, and by a congregation that has heard those stories and jokes before. They all seem to be asking, "What have you done lately?"

The temptation is to believe that life would be different or somehow better if we were always with those other people. Unfortunately, I can only keep the masquerade going for about three days; then my real personality starts to surface. If I stayed at the retreat center, it wouldn't be long before those people began to see me the way my family at home sees me. Then that same group of people would turn into my unavoidable world.

We are irresponsible when we withhold our involvement in order to avoid pain or frustration. We are irresponsible when we withhold involvement in order to avoid conflict. We are irresponsible when we make our world small in order to maintain control over ourselves and others. Finally, we are irresponsible when we fail to respond appropriately to the needs of our unavoidable world.

Irresponsible behavior probably doesn't begin with a decision to put up large, protective walls in our life. More likely, we start with small barriers designed to provide a little security or comfort from the pressures and pain of everyday existence. In time, these small barriers begin to form a relational wall that becomes a prison of isolation and emptiness. This is the antithesis of living by faith.

Irresponsibility is grounded in the conviction that *God is not able* to make a difference in our lives. We think, "He is not able to bring us through any trial or problem, pain or crisis or opportunity. He is not able . . . therefore I quit!" We miss what God would do in and through us, because we fall back in irresponsible behavior.

Overresponsible

Frustrating as it is to deal with people who are irresponsible, it is usually the overresponsible ones who drive us crazy. These hard-working folks are constantly trying to fix the world—their world, our world, someone else's world. Their battle cry is "Someone has to do something, or nothing will ever get done."

Unfortunately, this behavior often breeds passive dependence in others. A couple sat in my office locked in a bitter dispute. "He refuses to pick up his dirty socks and underwear. He just steps out of his clothes and expects me to pick them up and do the laundry like I'm a hired servant." When I asked her what she does about it, her response was "I always clean up after him; after all, he needs clean socks, and I don't want a messy house." That week I had them sign a contract stating that he would be responsible for his own laundry.

The next week I asked what had happened, and he said, "I left my clothes around as usual, and by the fourth day she gathered them up and washed them for me. I knew if I waited long enough she would take responsibility for me."

The next week she marched into my office with a big smile. What had happened? "He left his clothes around and I didn't touch them," she reported. "We even had company over and he had his old shirt and shoes in the living room through the whole evening, and I didn't touch them. By Thursday he had run out of clothes, so he went out and bought new socks. On Saturday he did the wash!"

Unhealthy dependence is broken when we have the courage to stop fixing everything. We are not God, and the sooner we realize it, the better off we will be. There can be a sense of glorified self-importance and power that comes with being over-responsible.

Sometimes our need to get involved helping or solving apparent problems has more to do with our own needs than with the issue before us. We're like the well-meaning Boy Scout who, seeing the older woman standing on the corner, insists on helping her cross the street, only to realize that she didn't want to cross the street. She was merely waiting for a bus. How many times have we jumped into a problem with good intentions only to discover that it really wasn't what it seemed to be?

Taking responsibility for others often keeps us from coming to grips with our own disappointments and needs. We all know pastors who throw themselves into the cares of the parishioners, only to dry up spiritually and relationally in the process; husbands and wives who devote their time and attention to the children and lose the love they once had for each other; businesspeople who sacrifice everything to build a career, only to lose touch with what life is all about; and political activists so obsessed with their particular cause that they become one-trick ponies, unable to relate in any other meaningful way.

Overresponsibility is as much a sin as irresponsibility. The message inherent in overresponsibility is "God is not able, therefore I must take action. God is not strong enough or smart enough or involved enough to make a difference, so it's up to me to make things happen." Our need to take matters into our own hands is ultimately rooted in our unwillingness to let God be God and to believe that He is able.

Responsival Living

Caught in the tension between selfish irresponsibility and selfish overresponsibility, we need a way to live that enables us to stand firmly in the gap between the need and opportunities all around us and God's loving presence and power to meet those needs. Unable to find a word that accurately describes the kind of responses Jesus is calling us to make, I decided to invent one. I call it "responsival" living.

To be responsival is to respond appropriately to the situation we face. It means being open to the world around us, aware of needs and opportunities, and in touch with our neighbors and their unique needs. To be responsival, we need to be honest about our own limits and inner resources, the circumstances that we have endured, the pains and struggles as well as the blessings we have known. It may require what Paul described in Romans 12, "taking a sober assessment of yourself, your strengths and weaknesses and gifts according to the faith given you." It may involve what many twelve-step programs call "a fearless moral inventory."

Finally, to be responsival is to be open with God. It is a response of faith to say, "He is able." Because Jesus Christ is alive and present in every area of our lives, we are equipped to face any family crisis, obstacle, need, or problem with confidence. This confidence is not in our ability but in the availability of God's resources.

God does not ask us to be strong enough, smart enough, or good enough for the situations we face in the unavoidable world. He wants us to realize that His strength is available to permeate our world and make a difference. All He asks is that we be responsival, that we look out at our world, that we look in at ourselves, and then that we look up to see what God can do in and through His family.

The unavoidable world can be a wonderful place. No matter how difficult life becomes, we belong in families. There may be times when we let down those we love and fail people who care the most, but through it all we discover a group of people who make us feel that we belong, who say, "What happens to you matters to me." Thus we stand together and face all of life with a confidence born of a sure identity in the family.

Don't be surprised by the fights, the laughter, or the tears; it's all part of life in the unavoidable world. When the worst happens, and we embarrass ourselves terribly, we know the freedom of belonging. John Cleese, in the movie *A Fish Called Wanda*, comments on the lack of freedom that often accompanies a British upbringing: "We British are so anal retentive, so stiff and proper, that we don't ask, 'How's your marriage?' for fear that you'll say, 'After ten years, it is finished.' We don't ask, 'How are your three children?' for fear of being told they all burned to death last Wednesday. We bear the fear of embarrassment."

In spite of the pain, frustration, and embarrassment, the unavoidable world of life in the family is still God's gift. The caring, nurture, and confidence that comes from being seen at our worst and still knowing that we belong is His gift to us. It is the place where we can practice responsival living and love one another over the long haul. It is a place where we see His power and grace demonstrated over and over again.

The unavoidable world can be a truly exciting place. In spite of the pitfalls, we meet Christ again and again. His love is let loose, so that our fears dissipate and we live in confidence.

CHAPTER SIX

Untidy Relationships

I was a man with a dilemma. I had fallen in love with the very beautiful and very blond Carol Reed, who sat across the room in Mrs. Brown's seventh grade English class. I was too shy to speak to her, or even look her in the eye, but I was passionately absorbed with the possibilities of a relationship with her.

Given my limited social skills and obvious nerdlike characteristics, I did what any committed Christian would do under similar stressful circumstances: I prayed about it! I prayed with earnest conviction, "God, you know how wonderful she is, and how much I care for her. You also know that I am too shy to approach her. I need a miracle, Lord. Please work in her heart so that she will call me on the phone and ask me to go steady. Amen."

I prayed about this situation faithfully for several months, until the fateful day. I got home from school just as the phone rang. When I answered it, a sweet voice said, "I'm Carol Reed. You may not know me, but I am in your English class." My head was spinning as I tried to make intelligent conversation (hoping to appear cool and calm as my heart beat out of control).

"I want to ask you something," she continued. "My sister is in Job's Daughters, and there is a big dance coming up at the end of the month. I wondered if you would be my date?" Could this really be happening to me? Before I could answer, she added the punchline. "All the girls are going steady with their dates, so if you went to this dance with me it would mean that we are going steady. Would that be all right with you?"

It had happened; God had answered my prayer. Carol Reed was on the phone asking me to go steady. My dream was about to come true. Softly I said, "I'm sorry, but I don't know how to dance." I hung up the phone. We never spoke to each other again.

I guess the lesson is that we should be careful what we ask for in our prayers. God is likely to answer them. I was afraid to appear clumsy or inadequate in this budding romance, so I missed the very thing I wanted most. I was too afraid to accept God's miracle in my life.

In our minds, relationships are wonderfully flawless opportunities to love and be loved. But in real life, they can be messy and confusing entanglements that are fraught with unexpected conditions that take us out of our comfort zones.

Relationships resist all attempts at tidiness. They are unpredictable, confusing, challenging, and often frightening. In spite of this, I am convinced that relationships are the litmus test of our faith. Jesus said, "By this will all people know that you are my disciples, that you have love one for another." Yet there has not been a more difficult aspect of Christianity than our relationships with one another.

One root of our relational struggles is a deep desire for control. Psychologists recognize that order reduces anxiety and that many people fend off stress by structuring their relationships in controlling ways. Some people have mistakenly seen control as a sign of maturity or spiritual growth. If we think God desires orderliness and control as a goal of discipleship, it follows that we will expend great effort to bring the people around us into a more controlled state.

Conflicts, tension, disagreements, differing perspectives are not encouraged because they create a sense of being out of control. Instead, we choose to align ourselves with people who are like us and who will reinforce our expectations about ourselves and our world. Relationships end up being a long attempt to mold others into our image. Rather than pointing people to Christ and encouraging conformity to His image, we seek to squeeze people into the molds of our expectations.

There is no denying that relationships can be uncomfortable. Perhaps there is no other time of life when we are more out of control than when we are in a relationship. We are plagued by unreal expectations about the other person as well as the relationship. Our own past experiences, hopes, primal fears, and inhibitions swirl together to confuse our desires and blur our motives. In a relationship there is nowhere to hide. We are thrust into a world of sharing and caring, knowing and risking, that might reduce even the most faithful disciple to a blob of quivering Jello.

Anatomy of a Relationship

Some people think that a relationship is what happens to two people who are waiting for something better to come along. Impulsive, unexpected, and intriguing adventures are these strange things called relationships. But whether the relationship involves a spouse, friends, small groups, churches, neighbors, or co-workers, there are similarities in the experience. Recognizing predictable stages in relationships can help us move toward one another as we grow toward intimacy.

Attraction

The initial attraction stage is filled with hope and uncertainty that is reminiscent of the old romantic song, "Some enchanted evening." This sense of wonder and attraction, mixed with a healthy dose of mystery and adventure, gives an unreal excitement to the initial phase of a relationship.

During this time, the person seems so fascinating and charming. Life appears more vital and intense. This is the stage

where we are seeking excitement, adventure, and affirmation.
Like the country western song, "Looking for Love in all the
Wrong Places" described, we scan the faces in a crowd hoping to
catch someone's attention and find the love we desire.

We search the eyes of strangers to see if we like how we
appear to them. In their eyes do we appear stronger, wiser, fun-
nier, or more spiritual? If so we will risk moving forward in the
relationship.

This first stage of attraction and discovery can be a marvelous opportunity for exploring and getting to know each other,
but the relationship often will remain undefined. Too much definition too soon may cause us to pull back from the other person
in order to maintain space, safety, and control.

Unfortunately, we cannot stay forever in the attraction
stage. Reality inevitably forces its way into a relationship. Expectations and limitations must be verbalized if we are to move
toward intimacy. Some people would prefer to skip reality and
move through a series of attractions. They relate to the old saying, "I'm giving up on reality and looking for a good fantasy."
But growing involves moving forward to commitment.

Commitment

Commitment occurs when people intentionally begin to define
the parameters of the relationship. At this stage they begin to
clarify what they will give and what they expect from their time
together. In order for a relationship to grow toward intimacy,
there must be definition. "Who am I to you?" "Are we a relationship?" "What can we expect from each other?" These and
other questions begin to form the understanding that allows for
a growing involvement between people.

Commitment cuts through our expectations, demanding
communication and clarity in the relationship. Problems occur
when there is a lack of clarity in the commitment stage. We may
assume based on previous experiences that people will respond to
us in predictable ways. Self-fulfilling prophecies are set in motion
when unspoken expectations go undiscerned.

Whether a new small group is forming, a person is joining a church, or a romance is budding, there comes a time for defining the relationship. Saying, "We are now in a relationship," points us toward growth, shared responsibility, and risk, as well as an opportunity for intimacy. It can be an incredibly frightening time, but also a time of new possibilities.

The Honeymoon

Once the initial commitment is made, a relationship can go through a relatively short period of time known (symbolically anyway) as the honeymoon. During this time of growth and exploration, the individuals are astounded at the incredible wisdom they demonstrated in selecting such fine companions for life's adventures.

Carefree bliss reigns as music swells and we dance in the meadow, discovering how much we have in common with each other. Every new experience is an opportunity to recognize our similarities. "He eats through his mouth, so do I!" "She likes me, I do too!" "We have so much in common!" Just being together is sufficient. People in this stage will go places and do things that under normal circumstances would be abhorrent. But if the other person enjoys it, that is enough for them.

In this stage we are often caught playing the "please me" game. We so want to make a good impression or be liked that we will set aside our own priorities and expectations in order to please the other person. "I will be for you what you want, and you be to me what I want." We tend to look into a person's eyes asking, "What do you want from me?" so that we can read the clues and fulfill the other person's expectations.

We may have learned this game early in life from significant adults who communicated, "I will only love you if . . ." We needed to be strong, perfect, quiet, or good in order for them to love us. Naively, we heard that message and determined in our hearts that we would earn their love. So we set out to be what they wanted us to be. Since they would only love us conditionally, we attempted to do what they wanted so that we could earn their love.

Inevitably, we failed and were not the perfect children that they desired. They withheld their love from us, making it appear to be our fault, since we weren't perfect. Undaunted, we pulled ourselves together and strove even harder. "Next time I will please them, then they will love me."

Now in adult relationships we seek out those clues that tell us what we must do to be loved. We want to know what the other person expects so that we can meet their expectation, thus proving our loveability. We don't realize that a relationship based on the "please me" game is doomed to failure and frustration. It is doomed because we cannot be perfect enough, strong enough, or good enough to earn anyone's love. The only way to win is by choosing not to play. Intimacy grows where we are free to care without reservation.

The Mulch Pile

Every relationship eventually hits the mulch pile. My grandmother kept a mulch pile in her backyard. She would pile up grass clippings, trash, and garbage from the kitchen, letting it all rot together until it turned into fertilizer. It probably was good for the plants, but it sure stunk up the neighborhood.

The Bandini Company in California is a large producer of steer manure fertilizer. Actually they don't manufacture steer manure so much as package and distribute it. The manure is still made the old-fashioned way. One of their very creative advertisements on television features a man dressed as a downhill skier, ready to descend a mountain—made entirely of steer manure. As the skier begins to glide down the huge pile of fertilizer, he falls on his face and rolls into the manure. The announcer says, "Bandini Mountain—man attempts to go where only cows have gone before."

This is the mental picture for many of us of what can happen as we move from attraction, commitment, and bliss into the hard realities of life in real relationships.

If everything was good in the honeymoon stage, now, on the mulch pile, everything is wrong. While it appeared that we had so much in common during the attraction part of our relationship, now we have nothing in common. The excitement that characterized the early stages of the relationship now gives way to monotony and predictability.

When people reach this stage, quirks of personality are suddenly transformed from interesting and amusing to grating and disruptive. Her "little smile" is now seen as a leering smirk. His spontaneity is now considered irresponsible and unreliable. The things about another person that we thought were charming little eccentricities are now full-blown deviant behaviors. The person whom we thought we knew so well now seems like a total stranger to us.

This same transition can be seen in group relationships as well. Have you been in a small group that initially began with intense excitement, clear expectation, and contagious joy as people shared together and allowed their lives to spill out in spontaneous sharing? When the group hits the mulch pile, there is a change in attitude toward the other group members, and everyone is open to criticism. The assertive member is accused of dominating the group process. The quiet member is accused of indifference and passivity. In this stage everything is wrong. Disillusionment is in the air, and it is easy to become frustrated with other people.

While the earlier stages of a relationship can be relatively brief, this phase tends to last a long time. Mulching tends to be a long, smelly chore. It is at this stage of a relationship that we are faced with the fact that relationships of any kind are an awful lot of work. We identify with Kris Kristofferson who sang with Rita Coolidge (his ex-wife), "Loving was easy, it's the living that's hard."

Intimacy

Intimacy is the result of coming through the difficult times of the mulch pile. Intimacy is the deep caring that results in sharing openly and honestly with someone in the trust that he or she will love you no matter what flaws and faults are mixed in with your strengths. At this stage, we no longer look for our value in the eyes of the other. Rather, it is sufficient to be known as the person we are.

Intimacy causes us to realize that the people who know and love us are not as impressed with us as peripheral people are. They don't panic if we are discouraged; they don't recoil from our anger; they don't overreact to our doubts and fears. There is an acceptance of us that shows itself in the realization that neither our happiest nor our worst moments will last forever. Thus patience and assurance through the ups and downs helps us to walk with surety through any circumstance.

Unfortunately, true intimacy only comes after the mulch pile. There is a misconception that intimacy can be found in the first three stages. Intimacy is linked to our ability to know and love unreservedly. We can only love someone to the extent that we know them. If we know a little bit about a person, we can love him a little bit. If we know him intimately, we can also love him intimately.

One of the characteristics of the mulch pile is that we cannot go over, around, or under it if we want to build a relationship that is deep and enduring. We must go *through* the mulch pile stage. Trying to miss the garbage in order to avoid pain will rob us of knowing intimacy. It can be incredibly freeing to discover that we are loveable in the very midst of the mulch pile, not only after we get through it. We find out that we are the givers and the receivers of a great love. At our best and our worst, we are loved. That, of course, is the essence of the gospel, in that "while we were still sinners, Christ died for us" (Rom. 5:8 NIV). God's love comes to us at times when we are least deserving and most unworthy.

There is nothing that provides more freedom and security than knowing that someone has honestly seen you without your protective walls and still loves you. A deeper, richer relationship can blossom from perservering in the mulch pile of real life.

Stay Away a Little Closer

Avoiding intimacy can lead to double messages in our relationships. We invite others to come toward us, while at the same time subtly fending off intimacy with a variety of psychological and relational weapons. Fear of drawing close to another person causes us to undermine the very relationships we seek. We avoid intimate relationships in order to avoid the mulch pile. In fact, it is possible to spend a whole lifetime avoiding intimacy.

Unfortunately, what often happens in a relationship is that we don't want to be hurt, so we erect walls of defense to protect ourselves. "I don't want her to think ill of me, so I won't tell her about . . ." "He might not love me if he knew about . . ." "The church won't respect me if they know about my struggle with . . ." One wall at a time, we erect barriers to intimacy.

Walls help us avoid the pain of the mulch pile. The result is that over time we become so relationally isolated and emotionally insulated that it is impossible to be known and loved intimately. We are also caught in the trap of having to maintain the walls that keep us from the secure relationships we desire most.

The only solution is to choose to take down the walls one by one. We need to make a conscious choice to move toward each other. Change begins when I risk removing a wall. This encourages the other person to remove one of her walls until we little by little allow the other to know us and love us without the protective barriers. This is risky. Our vulnerable behavior gives people knowledge that could be used against us. But even though being hurt is a definite possibility, taking the risk of vulnerability is our only hope if we are to experience intimacy.

Just because we're afraid people can't be trusted doesn't excuse our lack of vulnerability. Part of growing up is recognizing that people will let us down. They can't always be trusted to not hurt us. People will not always be there for us in the ways we want them to be. In fact, others are no different from you and me. We are no more trustworthy than anyone else. We will prob-

ably fail the ones we love. Knowing this, we can still choose to
be vulnerable.

The Long Haul

The enemy of long-term commitments is our preference for instant gratification. We have fantasy relationships in our minds
that ask for no investment, involve no risk. We merely show up
and experience being known, loved, valued, and nurtured. How
delightful! Too bad it is only a fantasy—this isn't the way it
works in the real world, because the essence of intimate relationships is not idyllic romance but hard work.

Working through the mulch pile toward intimacy requires a
commitment that propels us forward despite the circumstances
and without guarantees of success. There is no minimum wage
or retirement package in a love relationship. You can work hard,
give, care, share, and still not feel satisfied. Many of our relationships are like this one, described by a woman in a give-and-
take marriage: "I give, and he takes."

One of the deterrents to intimacy is the resistance we feel to
pain or discomfort in our lives. This avoidance of pain keeps us
from intimacy and results in a persistent lack of depth and understanding in relationships. Keith Miller has said, "Without
pain there is no wisdom." The avoidance of pain can result in
unwise choices for our lives.

The Liz and Dick Syndrome

I used to love reading about Liz Taylor and Richard Burton in
the movie magazines. They seemed to have a remarkable relationship that was characterized by falling in love with each other
over and over again. It was as if they did not like the mulch pile
stage of the relationship, so they would experience the first three
stages—attraction, commitment, honeymoon—then terminate
the relationship.

After going their separate ways, they would meet again across the crowded movie set, and the romantic sparks would fly once more. Each time they fell in love, they would get married again, honeymoon in an exotic locale, and become America's sweethearts once more.

When new problems surfaced, as they inevitably did, they would separate, divorce, and move on to other relationships. Then, unexpectedly they would meet again, and the cycle would repeat itself. Although they married and divorced each other several times, they appeared to seek without success that elusive intimacy that is only found at the end of the mulch pile. It seems tragic to be driven from the love we need by the fear we cannot face.

Avoiding commitments, we opt for new relationships that seem more exciting, in the hope that we will feel better about ourselves, at least for a short time. We move through this cycle in our romantic relationships, small groups, jobs, and even in our participation in churches. As soon as problems begin, when the feelings and excitement begin to fade in the shadow of reality, we move on to the new, hoping to find the missing ingredient or perfect person that will make our lives complete.

We have bought into the myth of the ideal relationship. In our families and in the church we have been encouraged to look for Mr. or Ms. Right. We look at relationships as if there may be a "right" person for us. We've believed the lie that there is someone out there who is just right for us. Someone who will love us in such a way that we will never have to change. We want relationships that are low maintenance, where we don't have to grow or stop destructive behaviors.

If we believe that there is a right person for us who will naturally accept us without conflict, then when we hit the difficulties of the mulch pile, we will recoil, thinking that the problem lies in picking the wrong person. We think, "No one is at fault, there is nothing to be done in the relationship, I merely chose unwisely." We end the relationship so that we can continue with our search for the right person, and we punish ourselves with another unsatisfying lap around the relational track.

Our desire to have a perfect relationship blurs us from see-ing people as they really are. We expect others to be perfect and pull away when we discover that they are flawed, blemished, not very charming or witty, sometimes dull, selfish, and immature. In fact, they are a lot like us. There are two questions we face: Are we willing to love someone who is imperfect? Are we willing to go through the mulch pile in order to discover intimacy?

Unfortunately for most of us, the answer is no. We will live without intimacy rather than face our fears and begin the painful process of changing. When we consider our options, it becomes obvious that we will not change until our pain becomes greater than our fear. As long as our fear of intimacy is greater than the pain of loneliness, we will try to hold out a little longer. Perhaps we would rather be in no relationship than in a difficult one.

The good news is that we don't have to be limited by our fears, as I was when Carol Reed asked me to the dance. There are fresh chances to enter exciting, challenging relationships every day. They will no doubt be untidy and probably lots of work, but it will be worth the effort.

CHAPTER SEVEN

Unmet Needs

*E*XPRESSING unmet needs to others can often be difficult. Sometimes when we ask for help, our words get tangled up in our swirling thoughts and emotions. A recent "Dear Abby" column offered the following excerpts from letters asking for help at the local welfare office:

> I am glad to report that my husband who is missing, is dead.
> Mrs. Jones has not had any clothes for a year and a half and has been visited regularly by the clergy.
> My husband got his project cut off two weeks ago, and I haven't had any relief since.
> I want money quick as I can get it. I have been in bed with the doctor for two weeks, and he doesn't do me any good.

We all have needs that at times go unmet. This can lead to a growing frustration. Sometimes a sense of hopelessness can creep into our hearts and leave us bitter or confused. Even though it's a common experience, we still find it difficult to express our needs, to ask for and receive help from others. Instead, we try to act strong so others will not suspect that we are feeling weak.

When I was a growing preteen, my father took me aside for the proverbial facts of life talk. He said there is one thing that I must keep in mind as I grow up and move out into the world: "Always pick up the check in a restaurant. No matter what the price, pay it and figure out how to cover the cost later. That way you will always appear strong."

I tucked that bit of fatherly wisdom into the recesses of my mind, until the memorable night when I was out to dinner with a large group of friends. It was a beautiful summer night. I was in a celebrative mood because I had just received my first paycheck from a new job at the surfboard factory, and I was trying hard to impress a pretty blond woman at the end of the table.

As our meal came to a close, the waitress brought the check, and everyone began to reach for their wallets and purses to pay their portion of the tab. Suddenly out of my mouth came a voice very much like my dad's, saying, "I'll take care of this, your money is no good here." Then with a grand gesture I picked up the bill and casually looked it over.

While everyone muttered their thanks and surprise at my show of generosity, I excused myself to the restroom where I splashed water on my face and worried about how I would pay for this dinner that totaled more than my entire paycheck. After some time, my friend Jim came to see what was keeping me, and he loaned me enough money to get out of the restaurant that night. It was painful, but I had passed the test of manhood. I had appeared to be strong. I picked up the check. Most of all, I had impressed the woman.

If we are to be authentic disciples, it is important to face our own neediness and move beyond appearances of strength. That will require us to understand what makes us resist appearing needy.

Perhaps one of the reasons that we choose to hide our needs is that we dislike being at the mercy of other people and their potentially hurtful responses. Face it, people often say things that are rude and embarrassing when we express a need. They try to either fix us or talk us out of our feelings or pronounce judgment on us. Rather than be treated like someone's project, it is easier to stay silent.

Another reason we may dislike sharing needs is that we are then forced to admit our own inability to maintain control of our lives. Control is an important element for us. To find ourselves out of control is a very frightening possibility.

Finally, it may be difficult to express needs because of the fear that these unmet needs are only the tip of the iceberg. If we expose our needs, we may unmask a much deeper problem of even greater discontent. Rather than face the hidden monsters within, we keep a lid on it, hoping that our unmet needs will just go away.

It is important for us to grasp the truth that there is no shame in neediness. For those of us who were raised to appear strong, neediness is a horrible condition from which we turn away. We don't mind giving generously or acting with compassion toward those who are needy around us, but we don't let ourselves get to the place where we must receive help from others. This fear of unmet needs can drive us to acquire, achieve, and accumulate symbols of satisfaction.

I remember a striking message in a recent advertisement in a magazine. An obviously successful businessman is sitting at a traffic signal in his brand new, beautiful Mercedes automobile. It looks at first glance like he has all the marks of status and achievement, but on closer inspection you see that he has a restless longing in his eyes as he stares out the window at the car next to him—a new Rolls Royce! The caption simply says, "When you have finally arrived . . ."

These symbols of satisfaction, while holding at bay our gnawing sense of insecurity and self-doubt, also can cloud our view of what is important. They may also inhibit our pursuing the very things we need most in life: relationships in which we are known intimately, in which we share vulnerably, and in which we discover love and accountability.

Just as there is no shame in being needy, there is also no shame in having plenty. Having plenty is neither a symbol of deep spirituality nor a trophy for faithfulness. For centuries people have used abundance as either an indicator of God's blessing (if it's my abundance) or a mark of corruption, abuse, and selfish exploitation (if it's your abundance).

Mission strategist Art Beals has pointed out a trap of responding to world problems out of a sense of guilt because we have so much. He calls it the paralysis of guilt. "If our response to the needs of the world is motivated by guilt over our apparent abundance then our response will be short lived and superficial."

Rather than obsessing about what we have or don't have, we need to discover the freedom that is ours when we realize that no obstacle or situation in life has the power to stop us from accomplishing that which Christ calls us to do. Our confidence lies not in what we have or don't have but in the realization of God's power releasing us to be the people we were created to be, to accomplish what we are called to do.

Whether our plate is full or empty is significant only to the extent that we allow Christ to be Lord of our life in either condition. Life's situations are merely the instances in which we are met by the One who knows our needs, loves us without reservation, and asks us, "Will you trust me this time?"

The Black Hole Syndrome

There are phenomena in our solar system commonly called black holes. One theory that astronomers have put forth to explain these unusual voids in space is that they are huge centers of negative energy. The "hole" creates a vacuum toward which other stars and planets are drawn. Eventually, they are pulled into the void at such incredible velocity that they finally cave in on themselves by the sheer force of negative energy.

It is possible for our unmet needs to function in the same way. When we have a need that is unmet, we can become so focused on that emptiness that we develop a negative energy that begins to drain away our strength, creativity, and resourcefulness. As we are pulled down by the vacuum within us, we find ourselves turning our attention inward, until we collapse from the pressure of negative energy.

We can easily get caught in the trap of defining ourselves by what we lack. Perhaps we feel that we missed out by having a dysfunctional family—we missed healthy parenting. Singles might begin to define themselves by their lack of a marriage partner and become preoccupied by the search for a mate. Married people think they are missing out on the independence and freedom of the single life, and they may become consumed in their desire for freedom. The same attitude that leads to focusing on our unmet needs may also stifle our ability to be thankful, and it may leave us feeling restless and discontented.

Consumption Orientation

We are becoming a nation of consumers. Our frantic attempts to fill unmet needs lead us to increasing levels of compulsive and obsessive behaviors. We consume food, alcohol, relationships, material goods, achievements, and even self-help books. Our thoughts become fixed on the things we lack, and we go to great lengths to try to fill the voids in our life.

Unfortunately, we are trying to fill the holes in our souls with things that were never created to meet those needs. When we feel lonely or depressed, we, like the Golden Girls on television, eat cheesecake. When we feel sad or angry, we might drink to fill the void. When we feel unappreciated and overlooked in our jobs, we consider having a sexual affair. These inappropriate behaviors lead to greater feelings of neediness, which lead to more inappropriate responses. If not corrected, the spiral of self-destruction continues unabated.

Our perceived needs often become an excuse for our sin. We try to rationalize our behavior by pointing out what is wrong in our life. It is as if we are justified in our sin because there is the pain of unmet needs. This is illustrated by country western singer Randy Travis in his song, "Reasons I Cheat":

A working day too long, where everything goes wrong.
A boss that don't know I'm alive.

I once had a notion I'd get that promotion,
but now I barely survive.
A wife too demanding, with no understanding
of why I'm dead on my feet . . .
The load that I carry, The dreams that I bury,
are some of the reasons I cheat.

My children keep growing, My age it keeps showing
Like all of the old friends I meet.
I'm growing older,
My life's growing colder.
That's some of the reasons I cheat.

When we begin the spiral of self-destruction, it is easy to grab onto things and try to make them excuses for our sin. Some people seem to think that just because they have needs that are unmet, they have the right to do anything they want in order to fill the void.

Sex, then, is reduced to the equivalent of a Big Mac attack. Remember the ad where normal folks would be driving down the road and suddenly feel a craving for a Big Mac? They would veer off the highway in their frantic effort to satisfy their hunger for a hamburger. In the same twisted way, we say, "I have unmet sexual hungers, therefore I must satisfy these hungers any way that I can." We destroy other people and ourselves in the process.

Like the whiny little girl, Veruca Salt in Roald Dahl's *Charlie and the Chocolate Factory*, we cry out, "I want it now, Daddy!" Our prayers become not dialogues where we discover God's agenda for us but merely another opportunity to go through our laundry list of dissatisfaction with our Heavenly Father. Our prayers in effect become childish tantrums in which we cry out to God, "I want it *now*, Daddy!"

Instant gratification can never lead to wholeness. The journey of discipleship requires that we move beyond instant satisfaction and the quick fulfillment of all unmet needs to the growing edge of delayed gratification, where we realize that all of our needs will not be met on our timetable, according to our plan.

We are confronted with the same prayer that Jesus prayed in the garden the night of His betrayal: "Nevertheless, not my will but your will be done."

As a young teenager, I was excited to see Mick Jagger and the Rolling Stones on their first American concert tour. They rocked the world and captured the pulse of a generation with their relentless, restless anthem, "I Can't Get No Satisfaction!" We, the baby boom generation, were hooked on the pursuit and achievement of satisfaction. But it was not to be found where we were looking.

Years later the Stones returned to the recording studios in England. Hard partying, drug addiction, personal conflicts, financial success, drug convictions, and the sudden death of a band member had changed their message. This time they rocked the world with a new song; "You Can't Always Get What You Want." Its message was that though many of our desires are unmet, we often get what we need.

Christian maturity requires us to face the reality that we will not be satisfied by the fulfillment of all our appetites. There will always be unfulfilled dreams and desires. Our task is not to fill all the holes but to allow God to use the circumstances and longings of our hearts for His purposes. In the process we look back and realize, like Paul, "My God will supply every need of yours according to his riches in glory in Christ Jesus" (Phil. 4:19 RSV). In other words, we can get what we need.

Our needs are the contact point for God's abundance. They can become the intersection where God and you collide—a head-on collision with grace, as God releases all of His riches to meet you at the point of your need, so that you can discover the joy of knowing Him and the contentment that brings.

CHAPTER EIGHT

Undivided Loyalty

W*E* are people who divide our loyalties. As the pressure of everyday living mounts, we find ourselves stretched to the limits. The incessant clamoring of people and constant demands for our time and attention lead us to lose sight of what is most important. For this reason, it is important to consider the issue of loyalty. Each of us has been called to have a relationship with God, to put Christ first in our lives. The Bible is filled with challenges to be undivided in our loyalty, but it is not easy to live that way on a daily basis.

Commitment is a two-way street. God commits to us, and we in turn follow Him. In Genesis 12 Abraham is invited to trust God. This is the beginning of the covenant relationship between God and His people. God bids Abraham to follow Him: to leave his home, land, comfort zone, heritage, and roots to go to a land that will be revealed to him. He gave up all those things that are sources of security and identity and received the promise; "I will be your God." This encounter is a foreshadowing of our call to walk by faith, trusting God when we don't know the final outcome.

In Exodus 20 the first of the Ten Commandments calls us to undivided loyalty: "You shall have no other gods before me. You shall not make for yourself a graven image or any likeness

. . . you shall not bow down to them or serve them; for I the Lord your God am a jealous God" (Ex. 20:3–5 RSV).

Joshua 24 gives us the challenge to the Hebrew people as they were about to enter the promised land: "Fear the Lord and serve him in sincerity and in faithfulness; put away the gods your fathers served and instead serve the Lord. If you are unwilling to serve the Lord, choose this day whom you will serve, but as for me and my house, we will serve the Lord."

In I Kings, Elijah challenges the people by saying, "How long will you go limping between two different opinions? If the Lord is God then follow Him, but if Baal is God, then follow him. And the people answered not a word."

Many people think that our loyalties are determined in the "important" moments of life. We look for big events that may alter our lives. However, very few of our most significant experiences happen in the big moments. More likely, we are shaped by the little things, the small commitments and actions, even those events that sneak up on us unexpectedly. We usually don't recognize their significance at the time, but in hindsight we realize their importance.

Some of us spend our time waiting for the big moment. When I was a teenager, the pastor at my church challenged the congregation with the proposition, "If you were brought before a godless Communist jury and charged with being a Christian, would there be enough evidence to convict you?"

This kind of challenge had the effect of making our faith seem unreal. It encouraged us to live our lives waiting for an incredible scenario to unfold so that we could make a stand for Christ. We needed to realize that all along the way we were making statements and taking stands for Jesus, without even knowing it.

Graven Images

What are our graven images? Unlike the people of the Bible, we don't necessarily have visible gods to worship, unless you are a surfer in Southern California; they used to have little wooden tiki gods that were supposed to bring good surf. Other than that, I don't remember having graven images in my life. We need to translate this phrase and ask what gods currently tug at our loyalty, leaving us spiritually paralyzed.

Work, for example, can become a graven image. Our jobs can be a source of great fulfillment and joy, or they can become a demanding god that we strive to appease. Some people would agree with Noel Coward: "Work is much more fun than fun." But Lily Tomlin reminds us, "The trouble with the rat race is that even if you win, you are still a rat."

Allegiance to our work can be a test of our loyalty. We are often expected to live, breathe, think, and dream only for the job. Otherwise we are reminded that there are at least ten other people who are waiting to take our place.

Wanting to succeed in the marketplace causes us to realign our values and priorities. In *The Addictive Organization*, Ann Wilson Schaef cites the tendency for companies to produce addictive behaviors in their employees. "The corporate culture supports workaholism, encouraging employees to become dependent on the company. In turn, workaholics use their jobs as a fix to get ahead, to be successful, to avoid feeling, and ultimately to avoid living."

I received a greeting card that was designed to look like an old horror movie ad. It said, " 'I am a rapidly aging workaholic!' The shocking confessions of a busy little bee who became a big barking beast. See the bloodshot eyes! Feel the weary bones! Hear the creaking back! Smell the fried brain! Featuring the ongoing hit theme: 'Get up, go to work, come home, go to bed . . . the extended version.' You can run out of brain cells but you can't hide!"

When our loyalties are out of order, we find ourselves bound to lesser things. There is an illusion of power for the person in bondage. I've never met an addict who didn't think he was totally in control. Even though the reality is that he lacks power in his life, he still feels and often appears very much in control.

I worked for a large corporation that had an 80 percent divorce rate for its managers. This may have been due to the fact that we lived totally for the company. I tried to make a statement for my faith by not working Sunday mornings so I could go to church with my family. I then would work the rest of the day and into the night, leaving my family at home alone every weekend.

Increasingly, people are faced with stressful relocations mandated by their employers. I remember being told on a Friday afternoon that I was to relocate to an office in a city 150 miles away. Over the weekend we had to find a place to live, move into our home, and be at the new office on Monday morning acting as if nothing extraordinary had happened over the weekend. To refuse to relocate would have sent a message that I was not a company man, and my future promotions would have been limited.

Meanwhile, I was having the time of my life. I was enjoying my job, making money, feeling powerful, in spite of the fact that my personal life was nonexistent, my marriage was in shambles, and my spiritual life was disintegrating. Work had become my graven image.

Love relationships can be graven images that demand our loyalty and attention. Sometimes the loyalty that we have to significant people conflicts with other loyalties. Commitments to friends and family can pull on us and further fragment our lives. George Burns once said, "Happiness is having a large, loving, caring, close-knit family . . . in another city."

Families are notorious for exerting pressure in order to gain our attention and remind us that they are a priority. Like the telephone advertisement, we call home and your mother says, "You never call." "But Ma," we say, "I'm calling right now." Undaunted, she responds, "How come you never call."

Part of living involves the process of letting go of former loyalties and embracing new ones. Our loyalties must shift as we grow and change. The psychological bonds that initially draw us toward people in time must be loosened so that new bonds can be formed with others. A counselor friend reminded me that before a person can marry, she must first get out of bed with her parents. This emotional separation is necessary in order for people to be free to form new loyalties and commitments.

Some people worship at the shrine of learning. It is possible to see education as an end in itself, rather than a preparation for what is really important. Education can consume us as we devote ourselves to the pursuit of a degree, knowledge, or grades, to the exclusion of finding balance in our lives. Expectations build up until we are unable to choose wisely in the face of mounting pressures. We lose the perspective that after college no one cares what our grades were. Al Maguire observed, "The world is run by C students." Though significant at the time, the importance of grades fades. They are merely one more way to keep score and reinforce or undermine our self-esteem.

Clothes and fashion can become a graven image that we embrace to give us power, status, and acceptance. Fashion consultant Robert Pante says what many of our lives echo: "If you look good and dress well, you don't need a purpose in life." Even so, it can be frustrating to have a little alligator on our shirts, only to discover that everyone else has insignias of guys playing polo. There was a time when the only name on my clothing was Fruit of the Loom. We can all take comfort from Oscar Wilde, who reminds us that "fashion is a form of ugliness so intolerable that we have to alter it every six months."

Our schedules can become graven images. We have increasingly seen schedule books take control of our lives. Have you noticed the increase of appointment books, time management systems, and computer-generated programs that monitor our lives? We tend to be people on the run. We are predictably fifteen minutes late for our next appointment. We are also usually a day or more behind on our projects. When we finally do sit down, it's to try to fit all the uncompleted things into tomorrow's already full schedule. We don't have time to stop for rest and evaluation, or recreation and renewal.

It's easy to become like little windup machines, drinking more espresso to keep going. While eating lunch, a friend said, "I feel like a little ant. From the moment I get up until I fall asleep at night, I am charging around doing endless tasks. Each one seems important and pressing at the time, but they may be no more significant than pushing breadcrumbs up the anthill."

Money or the lack of it can be a graven image. If we don't have enough money, we seek after it. If we have money, we obsess over keeping it or getting more. We worship it whether we have plenty or little—what a terrible pressure.

Worshiping lesser gods ultimately twists our values. Ivan Boesky, convicted of inside trading on Wall Street, once addressed the Stanford University School of Business and proclaimed, "Greed is good!"

The addictions that we use to avoid pain, create the illusion of power, and present false images, which join hand in hand with our greed. They ultimately leave us bowing before a graven image when we choose to be happy idiots in the pursuit of money and the pleasure it can buy.

Even the church can become a graven image. We can easily become overly involved in church activities. Soon we fall prey to pressure to conform and fulfill others' expectations. Ultimately we are no longer looking to Christ but to the church for our sense of security, fulfillment, and well-being.

When the church becomes a graven image, faithfulness gets reinterpreted as religious activity. Creative, life-giving ministry gives way to an endless round of church activities, committees, task forces, and meetings. "Doing church" begins to take precedence over "being the church." It doesn't take very long before we lose sight of the living, organic body of Christ. Instead of building the Kingdom of God, we find ourselves serving an organization that has no life.

The Cost of Undivided Loyalty

Standing in the bow of the shuttle boat, I could see the approaching harbor on Catalina Island. The quaint town of Avalon, only one mile square, was nestled peacefully above the water. On the outskirts of the village stood a large half-finished condominium project overlooking the sea. "That," the captain told me, "is what we call a developer's nightmare. The original builder ran out of money before the walls were completed, then it was sold to another builder, who lost his financing. A Canadian firm took over a few months ago, and they have just filed for bankruptcy." There, against the bluff was a giant monument to the builder's failure to count the cost.

Jesus asks us to consider the cost of discipleship before we commit to following Him. Are we willing to open our whole lives to Him? Will we allow Him to become Lord of every area of our lives? He wants to be Lord of our finances, careers, relationships, hopes, and dreams. He wants to be with us everywhere. Eventually all of our life is a reflection of His presence. It isn't enough to have a spiritual attitude apart from real life. He seeks to be Lord of our entire lives.

Counting the cost means that His agenda becomes our agenda. We can't say, "I have this figured out, Lord, so let me tell you how it's going to work. Looking at my schedule I think I can squeeze you in for a few minutes on Sunday morning." He wants His agenda and His priorities firmly planted inside of us. Sometimes that is hard for us to accept. After all, we think, "I have great ideas about how I think God ought to operate in the world, but He never seems to follow my advice."

Set Priorities

Plan according to your priorities and commitments. It's amazing how we can live in a way that is very different from the priorities we have established. For years I clearly stated my priorities as I saw them: "After God, my family is my priority." But my son asked me why, if he was such a priority in my life, did I always choose to go out to meetings rather than be with him. While my intention was to put him at the top of the list, it was easy to set him aside whenever there was something else crowding into my schedule.

People talk about priorities, but they are not always ex-pressed in tangible ways. Sometimes our priorities are set with-out conscious consideration. We live according to the "grumble theory": Whichever need grumbles the loudest becomes a pri-ority. So if my stomach grumbles, I'll go eat. If my wallet is grumbling, I'll go out and earn some money. If my social life is grumbling, it will get my attention. We need to be intentional and set our priorities according to our commitment to Christ.

When we observe ourselves in a number of situations, we begin to see what works for us. If we identify a top commitment, then it is helpful to examine ourselves and see if our time, energy, money, and interest flows to that commitment. Simply observing where our resources are flowing will tell us where our priorities really are.

It isn't enough to merely observe ourselves. We also need the accountability that comes from sharing with a few people the real issues of our lives. If it is difficult to make commitments and maintain undivided loyalties, we may need a group like Fence Sitters Anonymous that will help us to live according to the commitments we make.

While eating lunch with a group of elders and deacons from our church, I shared about my inability to spend quality time with my son. "There is just an endless stream of meetings and appointments that fill up the evenings and even the weekends. I'm afraid that he will grow up, and I will miss knowing him. We just don't have fun together."

As I was talking, an elder wrote on a piece of paper, then had it passed quietly around the table. When the paper reached me, I saw that it was a roughly drafted contract signed by each person at the table. It read, "I do hereby covenant with these brothers and sisters in Christ to not attend any meetings, gath-erings, or appointments on Sunday afternoons for a period of six months. Instead I will spend the afternoons with my son." There was a place for me to sign, right next to the signatures of ev-eryone at the table.

I was hesitant to make this commitment. I also felt a little miffed that they would intrude on my personal life. But I signed the covenant and headed for home, wondering what I had gotten myself into.

Later in the week, I received an envelope in the mail. Opening it, I found one adult and one child ticket to the aquarium in town. A note attached simply said, "Perhaps you can use these on Sunday." The next week I was sent tickets to the zoo. The following week there were tickets for the theater. These expressions of encouragement continued for six months; my friends were not only reminding me of our commitment, they also were enabling me to succeed at it!

If we share the tension of divided loyalties with a few fellow strugglers, we may unleash creative new ways to focus our lives. We need not carry on alone. We can be accountable to have more fun, balance, and joy in our lives. Allowing others to walk alongside as encouragers and fellow strugglers will lessen our pain and multiply our joy.

PART III

Broadening the Spectrum

CHAPTER NINE

Unconditional Love

*O*N Valentine's Day I received an interesting card. On it Cathy, the character from the comics, said, "Happy Valentine's Day to a man who is brilliant, sensitive, kind, thoughtful, generous, sexy, strong, wise, caring, gentle, passionate, noble, loving and perfect . . . At last, someone I have something in common with."

Isn't that what we look for in relationships? Whether romantic relationships, friendships, a small group, or a church, we want to be with people who will help us look better or feel better about ourselves. We have an image of the kind of person we would like to be, then we seek out individuals or groups or ministries where there will be people who might enable us to feel more healthy and whole. We spend a lot of time and energy seeking out these people who will help us feel better about ourselves, but when we get close we see that they only measure a nine on the scale of one to ten, so we move away from the relationship, drifting on to someone or something else that is more perfect for us.

I was struggling in my relationship with a person at church. I wanted to be loving but didn't know what to do. Finally, in desperation, I asked my pastor, Bruce Larson, what the loving response would be in this situation. His response was "It's hard to tell, no one knows the shape of love." Sometimes what appears to be loving is clouded by mixed motives and hidden agendas. There are dangers below the surface in every relationship. The loving response may not be that obvious. Relationships rarely fit the pattern of our preconceived ideas. They will inevitably find ways to break out of the molds we set up for them.

As Jackson Browne expressed in his song "The Shape of a Heart," it is much easier to speak of love than to live it. We work hard at loving others never realizing how treacherous it can be to navigate the waters of a relationship.

We don't know what the other person is talking about or what her unmet needs or secret longings consist of. We spend time talking, sharing, fighting, growing, all the while expecting the relationship to be easy. If it is not trouble free, we fear that something is wrong either with us or with the other person.

In time we move on to another person, or another group, or another church, seeking problem-free relationships. But as new difficulties become apparent, we move on again, never experiencing love that is unconditional.

There is a great and desperate need to discover unconditional love. We need to love in a way that only God makes possible for us. The pitfall is that when we see the biblical model for love, we settle back, realizing that we fall short of God's standard and we think it is impossible for us to love in that way.

Perhaps the starting point is to not try to conjure up a loving feeling or aura of perfect love, but rather to start with the relationships we are in and behave lovingly in them. We can't force ourselves to love someone unreservedly and unconditionally—feelings come and go. But we can change our expressed behavior and begin to act in loving ways, hoping that the emotional response will follow.

The Shape of Love

Paul's attributes of love in his letter to the church in Corinth help us understand love. He begins by writing that love is patient. If

I were making a list of my own behaviors, patience would prob-ably not be at the top of the list. Like many of you, I prefer instant gratification in my relationships. Maybe we are drawn to short-term superficial relationships because we don't have to take many risks in them. We can present ourselves any way we desire, keeping up an image rather than being real with each other. We can remain in control of the relationship as long as it remains on our terms.

But real love is discovered over the course of a long-term relationship. It is patient, taking time to grow, change, adjust, and unfold in a trusting, safe environment. Patience takes place beyond the superficial, where we are seen for who we are and who we might become by God's grace. Patience gives us room to grow and change so that we don't give up on others simply because they are not what we want them to be, or because they fail us.

It is sometimes difficult for me to live with delayed grati-fication. I struggle with the long viewpoint in many areas of life. It is always more fun to have the instant result, and the gratifi-cation that that brings. So I'd rather make new relationships each day, starting over and beginning again. I'd prefer to join a new small group rather than struggle through the doldrums of the old group. But to follow my inclinations would leave me unable to know love over the long haul. I'd miss out on love that is patient.

Love is kind. It takes pressure without lashing back, without plotting the next attack. Kindness is not a passive response to a situation. It is an active, aggressive pursuit of doing the kind behavior even if we don't feel like it. There are people who are genuinely kind, and they have become heroes for me. It is fun to watch them in situations where I would not be kind; they express a graciousness under pressure that astonishes me. They actively pursue kindness regardless of the behavior of the other person. Love has nothing to do with what another person does or doesn't do, or how he responds to us, or if he is living up to our expectations. Rather, it has to do with what we are going to do with each other.

Love is not jealous. There is a link between jealousy and hatred. The word used in the Bible meant to boil with envy and hatred as if the two were mingled together. What is it about jealousy that links it with hatred? To be jealous is to long to be where someone else is, to have what someone else has, to be who someone else is. The logical next step results in our hating the other person for having what she has or for being who she is.

The root of jealousy is the fundamental disdain of who you yourself are. The reason you are so angry at the other person is that you are so dissatisfied with who you are. Love is destroyed because we drive ourselves further and further away, with the destructive self-hate of jealousy. When we are in this cycle, we play the comparison game with others.

Unfortunately, the church is probably a place where comparison is practiced more than anywhere else in our world. One of the saddest things I hear is that people are afraid to go to church because it appears as if everyone has it completely together and is strong, confident, and self-assured. Thinking this is the case, people recoil, thinking that they don't have what it takes to fit in. The reality is that behind these handsome surfaces we would find that most everyone struggles with very similar difficulties and that we have more in common than it would appear at first glance.

Imagine how hard it is to attend church if you don't have a job you are proud of. If you were laid off this week or last year, or if you are still looking to find a job, if you are in a job that is unfulfilling or that you are embarrassed to tell others about, it is very uncomfortable to be in an environment where you have to lie, cover up, or stay home.

The *Wall Street Journal* once ran an article entitled "Style vs. Substance." Research done by American Sports Data, Inc., reported that only about half of the adults purchasing athletic apparel participated in the sport the apparel was made for. Fifty percent of all buyers of tennis shoes don't play tennis and don't own a racket. Forty-nine percent of those buying running shoes don't run at all. Forty-three percent of those buying leotards never work out in them. We want to have them, want to buy them, want to wear them around in conspicuous fashion, but we use them more to create an image about ourselves than for the purposes for which they were created. This practice only feeds the fires of jealousy, contributing to the negative whirlpool that draws us down, and undermines our ability to love.

Love is not boastful or proud. There are many ways to express pride. Intellectual pride leads us to make comments that communicate, "See how smart I am; see how dumb you are." Our boast seems to have a flip side. While we are making a statement about ourselves, we are also making a statement about the other person that tends to be equal and opposite in meaning.

Proudness implies puffing ourselves up. In effect, we look like pigeons, who puff up their feathers in order to strike an impressive pose. When we were teenagers, my brother Richard raised pigeons. It was fun to watch them fluff out their feathers, throw back their heads, and strut around the coop as if to say, "Notice me, I'm really something." I was less impressed by their little display than some of the other pigeons were. Perhaps God looks at us unimpressed, as if to say, "Why are you posing and posturing for each other like that?"

Placing importance on our ability to look good, strong, and in control results in our killing the very love we seek. Even as we puff up and strike poses for one another, we work to keep the image up in order to impress and win the love, acceptance, and approval we seek. But we can't maintain the image for very long. We move on before our real size is apparent.

Jesus spoke about the pompous person in the temple whose prayer was "Thank you, Lord, that you made me the way I am, not like this other person." We make similar prayers as we look around and compare ourselves with others in order to make ourselves appear better. Kris Kristofferson wrote a song that reveals the problem of the comparison game:

Everybody's got to have somebody to look down on.
Someone doing worse than them at any time they please.

Someone doing something dirty, decent folks can frown on.
If you don't have someone else, then help yourself to me.

Meanwhile Jesus said, "The other man without looking up said, 'Have mercy on me, a sinner.' " One person walked out of the temple forgiven and restored, while the other walked out empty. Which one was which? If we are to discover the power of unconditional love, we must set aside the tendency to puff ourselves up with inappropriate expressions of pride.

Love is not rude. Unfortunately, rudeness is within the domain of the church, to the extent that many people have asked why non-Christians are more polite and gracious than are professing believers. Perhaps as believers we believe that our grasp on truth gives us permission to say or do whatever we want in relationships without regard for the feelings and character of the people we relate to. Rudeness in the name of Christ is never love. There is no such thing as holy rudeness.

Rudeness can be expressed in many ways. It can be the failure to tune in to the other person, or it can be the inflicting of ourselves on them. It is ultimately relationship destroying, because we treat others as objects on whom we inflict ourselves. Perhaps it is bred in the familiarity of church relationships. Sometimes we excuse ourselves by quoting Jesus' admonition to "speak the truth in love." Whatever the reason, rudeness is rampant.

There is a desperate sense that we need to be heard, listened to, or taken seriously as we strive to change other people. We put the focus not on ourselves but on others. We mistakenly think that if they were different, then we would be different. If they were more open, then God could do something; if they were more loving, then we'd feel loved and nurtured. But if they won't change, it is up to us to tell them what they must do to change.

I hear rude comments on a regular basis. Unfortunately, people will say rude things to people in the church that would never be said to strangers on the street. Personal comments, observations about appearance, behavior, or life-style, all are legitimate when rudeness is on the prowl. Love cannot grow and be fostered in an environment of rudeness. Rudeness is a clear expression of disregard. In effect, we are saying that the person to whom we are being rude doesn't matter to us. We reduce one another to objects of disdain.

Love is not selfish, insisting on its own way. I was a master in my marriage of having a better way to do things. In the early years, no matter what Eileen wanted to do, I had a better way. Whether the issues were large or small didn't matter. I had a better way to shop for groceries, drive the car, pack a suitcase. I even had a better way to cook spaghetti and boil water. She finally gave up after 15 years, and now I do much of the cooking. Our kitchen ceiling is now covered with spaghetti from my flinging it up to see if it sticks (so I will know it is ready).

My desperate need to be right almost killed her love for me. In the process I learned that I had to choose between my need to be right and a loving relationship. It isn't possible to have both.

The same thing holds for group relationships. Sometimes when people share in small groups, they are met with responses that reek with "better way" messages. We revert to trying to fix one another rather than listening and supporting. We end up debating biblical interpretation rather than ministering to the real needs of our fellow strugglers.

The result of this kind of behavior is that we begin to train others in our lives to be passive around us. It really doesn't matter what they say or do, so they back off, letting us have our way, but the love begins to evaporate. When we have to win or have to be right, we do it at the expense of love.

Love isn't irritable. I've noticed that there are people who seem to be waiting to be offended. Some folks keep alert to see if they can detect something that will offend them. These are the people who will watch other people's lives, hoping to find something wrong that will somehow justify the negative attitude they already hold. Thus our actions lead to the fulfilment of their predetermined expectations.

Hurts and resentments that are stored away will inevitably block the love we seek. When we hold in resentments, we fall victim to the garbage pail of the past that we carry with us. Rather than disposing of the hurts, we end up carrying them with us, like giant garbage bags on our backs. Whenever we are hurt or angry or sad, we stick that feeling into the bag and keep it until a future time when we have opportunity to express ourselves. Then out come all the bad feelings and resentments that have been stored away, a discharge that leaves us neither healed nor forgiven.

Many of us kill love by carrying around these garbage bags of the past. Wouldn't it be wonderful to have an automatic garbage disposal in our relationships? That way, when hurts come or we are let down or disappointed by those we love, we could take it, acknowledge the pain, and then rid ourselves of the negative matter.

In the book *The Postponed Generation*, which is a study of persons who in today's world are putting their lives on hold, it is demonstrated that people are making decisions about ten years later than folks in the previous generation made them. Earlier generations, during the ages of 18 to 22, were making career choices and deciding on marriage, where they would live, and what they would do with their lives. Now those decisions have been pushed up to the ages of 28 to 32 and beyond. One person interviewed said, "I have too many choices, I'm waiting for my niche to find me. There is just no market for the renaissance woman anymore."

Author Susan Litwin says,

> Today's young adults are just victims of social change, their personality as a generation, make them very much part of it. Commitment to a relationship for them is just as difficult as commitment to a career or to a point of view or to a lifestyle. It is one more act that might define them, and therefore limit their potential.

Litwin continues,

> "I asked Ellen, a young actress I met if she planned to marry the man she is living with. "I'm still looking for the perfect man and the perfect relationship, even though I know it's a fantasy." She

cannot say what is imperfect about this man, and she seems to be in love with him, but to say "this is it," is limiting. It is an admission of adulthood.

Besides its difficult to be in a relationship if you still don't know who you are. There is a tendency to demand too much, depend too much and be dissatisfied for vague reasons. What we want from the other person is not company, but an identity.

It is so hard to have the kind of relationships that are marked by unconditional love, because our identity is on the line in them.

When we postpone adulthood, trying to prolong adolescence, it is difficult to love meaningfully. Songwriter Jimmy Buffet creates an aura of prolonged adolescence with his song "Margaritaville," which romanticizes the life of a beach bum whose biggest concern is finding the salt shaker, so he can mix another drink.

His music lures our longing to be free and unfettered. Sounding like one big midlife crisis, his lyrics touch that part of us that wants to put off maturity as long as possible by rekindling the excitement and thrill of irresponsibility.

Responsibility is too often seen as something for others to live out, not for us. There is a shift in attitude that comes when we realize life is more than procrastination and parties. Making choices that help determine who we are and what we will become is an essential step in growing toward maturity. It is in the context of these decisions that we discover the essence of love.

I was nervously waiting outside of the doctor's office. Eileen and I had been engaged for several months, but something was very wrong. Her health was failing; she was increasingly frightened and prone to severe anxiety attacks.

Feeling a little bit nervous, I entered the office and sat down. The doctor looked me in the eye and stunned me by saying, "Get out of her life, or you will destroy her—you are incapable of loving anyone!"

Perhaps I had behaved in ways that were domineering, volatile, demeaning, and emotionally abusive, but maybe he was overstating how unloving I really was. "I can change. Really, I will try to be different."

"You can't change," he told me. "Just go away."

Sitting alone in my apartment that night, I considered what the doctor had said. Alternately, I felt sad, angry, and hopeless. Most of all, I felt helpless. The problem could not be blamed on anyone else. The enemy had been identified, and it was me. I was not a loving person. I didn't know how to love unconditionally, and I seemed intuitively to do the things that were most destructive in my relationships.

Not having anyone else to talk with at the time, I began to talk with God. I told Him about the confrontation with the doctor, and the terrible realization of my inability to love. I admitted to Him that the doctor had been right; I couldn't seem to act loving, despite my intentions. Then I asked if somehow He would begin to love Eileen through me, allowing me to begin to demonstrate the characteristics of love, even if it went against my naturally abusive tendencies.

Something began to change in me. I wasn't instinctively kind, patient, or gracious, but I was starting to act differently. I found myself not saying the demeaning insults that before had so easily rolled out of my mouth. I ceased beating her spirit down with my willfulness. I began to treat her with respect instead of disdain.

It was a small beginning step, but it was a turning point for me. Unconditional love is no longer an abstract concept or spiritual principle. Rather, it is God's intervening gift to make us healthy and whole people.

CHAPTER TEN

Unexpected Joy

RECENTLY, the radio airwaves were filled with the easygoing sound of a popular song admonishing, "Don't worry, be happy." Most of us, I assume, would like to be happy. Unfortunately, happiness is not a guarantee in life. In fact, a Spanish proverb reminds us, "There is no happiness, there are only moments of happiness." Either way, I hope you have your share of happy moments. I'm convinced that given a choice between misery and happiness, we'd probably be better off with the latter.

Happiness, like many other emotional responses, is a reaction to the circumstances we experience. How we react can depend on choices we've made and attitudes that we carry about ourselves, others, and God.

No matter what clever songs we listen to or what we do to be positive and face the world with a smile, there are many things that seep in and erode our efforts to be happy. Disappointment and stress can undermine our attitudes until we react in strange and unexpected ways. We develop arsenals that include both good and bad strategies to handle stress when it surfaces in our life.

Some people deal with stress by lashing out. When things get bad, the frustrations build, and the pain becomes severe, they

resort to taking it out on someone else. I recently heard the story
of a man in Enumclaw, Washington, who used a bulldozer to rip
apart his family's new home while his wife was out of town.

> "We separated last summer and on Monday I filed for divorce,"
> the wife told reporters. "I told him that I wanted to keep the
> house. I guess he didn't want me to have it." The home which
> looked as if it had been hit by a tornado, had been smashed to the
> ground with both a bulldozer and a backhoe. An Enumclaw police
> officer said the case was under investigation but that the police
> might not have much to do because the husband had obtained the
> $11.50 demolition permit from city hall.

An article in *USA Today* reports,

> Frustrated drivers are sweet on the Revenger. One of this sea-
> son's hottest adult toys offers frustrated drivers caught in traffic
> jams a way to vent their feelings when someone cuts into their
> lanes or turns without using a signal. The toy, shaped like a radar
> detector and mounted on the dash board, blasts the sounds of
> grenade launcher, machine gun or death ray! People are connecting
> these to outside speakers, bull horns and citizen band radios.

A recent ad in a Los Angeles magazine encouraged readers
to think of a loved one who broke your heart, or the boss that
refused to give you the raise you deserved, or the stockbroker
who convinced you to invest days before Black Monday. What
was the product they were selling? Personal voodoo dolls complete with torture implements and instructions. These have become best-selling gifts for frustrated and overstressed executives.

While some people handle stress and disappointment by
lashing out, others pretend everything is fine. Some cope by
blaming others and making excuses for themselves. We can go
through our whole life making excuses, or we can find a different
way to live. We need a new strategy that results not just in
happiness, which is transitory, but in a true experience of joy.

Unlike happiness, joy is not linked to our circumstances.
Neither is it as fickle as our emotional reactions. Rather, it
emerges as a result of the Holy Spirit's presence in us. Joy allows

us to respond to life without reacting. It is a gift from God that enables us to transform ordinary situations into something extraordinary.

Jesus said, "These things I have spoken to you that my joy may be in you, and that your joy may be full" (John 15:11 RSV). This fullness of joy eludes even the most committed Christians. We in the church have exchanged the experience of joy for the weight of religion. Taking ourselves too seriously, we seem to have misplaced our laughter. When I'm around people who are missing the joy in life, I think of Oscar Wilde's words, "Seriousness is the last refuge of the shallow."

There may be no more important work for a follower of Christ today than the bearing of joy. My son's kindergarten teacher told me that a child's work is to play. Perhaps we as Christians need to see our work to be the playful exercise of joy.

Where Did the Joy Go?

Perhaps one reason for the lack of joy within the church is the large number of church attenders who have never had a personal relationship with Jesus Christ. The church is reduced to a community center or a service organization when its members haven't responded to Christ's invitation to follow Him. These fine, upstanding, moral, nice people have yet to get to the point where they say yes to Jesus. They must reach a point of need that is so great that they recognize it's time for a change of allegiance within themselves.

The result of this phenomenon is that our churches are filled with well-meaning people who are attending worship, taking classes, and participating on committees and task forces without Jesus Christ being alive in them. In effect, we have people who are growing and serving without having been born. This is as tenable as teaching an unborn child how to walk. Is it any wonder why we seem to lack power and peace and joy in our daily lives?

The Christian life is impossible to live apart from the indwelling presence of Jesus as the center of one's life. The Christian life was never meant to be lived apart from Jesus Christ. This is but one more way that we try to live according to our own terms. But it doesn't work, and the result is a noticeable lack of joy.

Another reason that we lack joy is a fundamental misunderstanding of the nature of discipleship. Discipleship is the lifelong process whereby we allow the Lord to work within us to shape us into His image. As we walk with Him, we become more like Him as well as becoming more unique ourselves. Learning, growing, risking, and changing are all part of the process by which we become yoked to Christ.

While vacationing in New England, my family and I visited Sturbridge Village in Massachusetts. It was fascinating to see a whole town as it might have been in Colonial times. During the late afternoon, we watched teams of oxen working in the fields. The oxen were yoked together as they pulled a plow behind them, with the farmer following to the side.

A nearby villager explained that they yoke together a mature, strong ox with a younger, less-developed ox to make a team. They understand that two young inexperienced oxen would be unable to carry the load and would create a difficult steering problem for the farmer. The older large oxen are less prone to veer off the path and are able to carry the weight of the yoke as well as the load. They also will resist the willful impulses of the young inexperienced oxen. Gradually the younger ox grows stronger and larger and is developed into a productive working partner. It's like a "be all that you can be" program for oxen.

Leaving Sturbridge Village, we traveled up the coast of Maine, where I found an antique ox yoke hanging in the dining room of an old inn. After some negotiations, I bought the yoke and smuggled it onto the airplane, disguised in a garment bag.

Arriving home, I anticipated hanging the yoke on the wall of my office. It might serve as a daily reminder that a young, headstrong, undeveloped ox is gently strengthened, guided, and directed by a stronger ox who walks beside him. It seemed at first glance to be a vivid picture of the discipleship process in which we are strengthened, guided, and corrected when we veer off in our own direction. Wherever we go, Christ is right beside us. He is yoked to us in our homes, in our work, in our play, and at church. It is an inseparable relationship because we are yoked together.

Suddenly I realized that the ox yoke is not like the yoke of discipleship Jesus offers to us. It is more like the yoke we carry before we meet Christ. It is the burden of life that weighs us down as we strive to live according to our own will and strength. When we come to Christ, He invites us to remove the heavy, rough, burdensome yoke we carry and leave it behind for the yoke He brings.

Looking at the antique yoke, it is obvious that it is incredibly heavy. At first glance it appears to be made entirely of cement. It is hewn from a single beam and weighs well over one hundred pounds.

Besides being heavy, it is very rough. The surface is hard and ruggedly textured so that it would chafe and wear down the skin that comes in contact with it. It is also functional—oxen won't wander away, wearing this piece of timber around their necks. It fulfills the task it was made to accomplish.

Jesus said, "Take my yoke upon you and learn from me . . . for my yoke is easy and my burden is light" (Matt. 11:29, 30 NIV). The old, rough, hard, and heavy yoke is not what Christ has for us. During the years He spent working in the carpenter shop, He probably made a few ox yokes, so He understood what was involved. The yoke He brings to us has a custom fit, because He knows our needs as well as our strengths. He knows us because He made us, so the fit is perfect. Moreover, His yoke is light because He is the one who bears the weight on our behalf. In the process we grow stronger as He walks next to us. We become more confident as His spirit infuses us. We become Christlike: strong, loving, and joyful.

We've made a terrible mistake. Rather than grasp the implications of following Jesus Christ, we have developed a discipleship model that is based on quality control. There are constant reminders that we are doing something wrong. People are quick to share their opinions about how we can change to be better, stronger, and more spiritual. Christianity has become a continuous reminder that we are not measuring up. We need a new model of discipleship that results in joy.

On our last day in New England, we stopped for the tour of the Ben and Jerry's Ice Cream factory. We heard the fascinating story of Ben and Jerry, two college dropouts who sent away for a five-dollar mail order course on how to make ice cream. After only a few short years they were the third largest producers of gourmet ice cream in the world.

As their company grew, it became apparent to the two partners that their jobs had ceased to be fun. Work and its ensuing responsibilities were robbing them of their zest and creativity. According to the tour guide, they began to assess their company and determined that they were not in business to sell ice cream but to create joy.

Realizing their purpose, they hired a person to serve as Director of Joy for the company. The job consisted of planning fun activities and celebrations for the company and the community. Large stereo speakers were mounted in the factory so that loud party rock and roll would blare over the assembly lines. Believing that they were in the joy business, they set aside 7½ percent of pretax profits for charities, festivals, community service, and special causes.

A problem arose on the assembly line when "Cherry Garcia," a new flavor named after rock star Jerry Garcia of the Grateful Dead, was introduced. Though they used pitted cherries, pits were still getting past the workers and ending up in the ice cream. They set to work to find the solution to this problem.

Resisting the quality control mind-set that would punish workers for letting pits slip by, they came up with a new strategy. The workers would be paid their regular salary for seeking out the pits. But for every pit they found, they would receive a bonus of one dollar. In other words, they paid them for doing their job, then gave them a bonus when they did it. The result was amazing; fewer pits got into the ice cream, and the employees loved to work on the "pit line." Creative problem solving brought joy to everyone.

When Ben and Jerry discovered that the chocolate chunks used in another ice cream were too large to go through their packing machines, they were tempted to conform to industry standards and make smaller chunks. Instead, they got creative and found an old abandoned cottage cheese machine in a nearby dairy farm. The machine could handle large curd cottage cheese, and soon it was handling the extra-big chunks of chocolate.

If joy is our product, we are free to find new, creative ways to serve and encourage one another. When the stock market plummeted on Black Monday, panic and desperation were everywhere. Ben and Jerry were on the sidewalks of Wall Street scooping out free bowls of "Economic Crunch" ice cream.

Perhaps as Christians we can learn something from these two ice cream entrepreneurs. Have we lost sight of the product of our faith? We have missed the joy by acting like quality control advisers for one another. What would happen if we exchanged our yoke of quality control for a new, lighter yoke of joy? The old heavy one doesn't seem to work that well anyway. Besides, joy is what the yoke of Jesus Christ is all about. "My yoke is easy, my burden is light," Christ tells His disciples. If we are feeling overburdened, it is time to trade in the old yoke on a newer model.

We are Directors of Joy. This means that problems and obstacles can be looked at in fresh new ways. Our viewpoint is not how to tighten our fists and work harder. Neither is it to exact a higher standard of behavior from those around us. Rather, we are challenged to discover how we can do something wild and carefree that nurtures joy.

What would you do differently in your home if you were the Director of Joy? Imagine receiving a promotion at work to vice president in charge of joy. Where would you start? What could be different if joy was the product? What would you do if your church called you to be Pastor of Joy? Sound impossible? Maybe the time has come for a fresh start.

CHAPTER ELEVEN

Unforgettable Adventure

*T*HE city of Seoul was just waking up. Due to jet lag, I had been up for hours. My adventuresome spirit was aroused, so I grabbed a few of the church leaders who had traveled to South Korea in our group and invited them to explore the city with me as their guide.

Brad, an attorney, was hesitant at first. "We have to be back for a meeting by 8:30. Besides, this is a large city with millions of people, political unrest, and we don't speak the language," he reminded us. "Are you sure you can get us back safely?" Responding with more bravado than intelligence, I smiled and said, "Trust me!" Off we went on our adventure.

Strolling through the winding backstreets of the city, our senses were alive with sights, sounds, and smells that were all so strange to us. It was fun to watch impromptu markets being set up along the streets as schoolchildren and adults streamed by us on their way to class or work.

It was all so interesting that I lost track of the time until Brad, the attorney, reminded us that it was getting late, and we really should head back now. "Don't worry, I'll get you back in time for the meeting. I know what I'm doing, just trust me," I chortled. On we went.

After a few more minutes of wandering, the group stopped and demanded that I tell them how we would get back to our hotel in time. With a sense of smug resolution, I pointed up the street to an alley. "We will go left up that alley; it will circle around and drop us off right at our hotel," I told them confidently. They were suitably impressed with my innate sense of direction, commended me for my leadership, and boldly followed me up the street.

At the alley we turned left and proceeded to follow an increasingly narrow path that curved not to the left as I had assumed but more and more to the right. The incline grew steeper as we climbed higher and higher, in the wrong direction. Someone pointed out that the cute shops and quaint stalls were gone, and the residences were becoming more sparse as we climbed what was beginning to feel like a mountain. It appeared that we were leaving the city of Seoul and heading out into the countryside. I had to admit we were lost.

The group gave me one of those "We will never trust you again" looks. I turned to the attorney and asked if he could help us find our way back to the hotel. He led us back the way we had come, and our hearty band of misguided adventurers finally arrived at our quarters.

Life is filled with people who readily say "Trust me." But there is good reason not to trust when the person we follow cannot show the way and bring us safely through to our destination. When Jesus bids us to follow Him, He says, "trust me," and we can be confident that He is able to complete what He calls us to accomplish.

In order to experience the unforgettable adventure that the Christian life offers, we must put our trust in the One who will not let us down. We must learn to trust Christ in tangible ways.

While at a convention in Atlanta, I was approached by Richard, the shoeshine man. I told him I didn't want a shine, but he said he would shine my shoes for free. "A shoeshine for a tip, that's the best deal in town," he told me. Not the kind of person to pass up a bargain, I climbed up on the chair while Richard worked on my shoes.

When he was finished, I started to get up, but he said, "Wait a minute, it's time for your tip." Confused, I sat back down, and he reminded me, "Shine for a tip—now I have a tip to give you."

He asked me if I trusted God with every area of my life. I said that I do most of the time. Then he told me to picture a construction worker building a tall office complex, who suddenly slips and falls. He finds himself hanging to a scaffold, desperately, many floors above the pavement. Fortunately, God is standing on the sidewalk below, and he calls out, "Let go of the scaffold, and let yourself fall. Trust me; I love you and I will catch you." While the worker is thinking this over, the devil suddenly appears next to God and yells, "Hang on, brother, don't let go!" Richard looked me in the eye and asked, "Who are you gonna trust, mister?"

I paid for the shine and walked away thinking about Richard the shoeshine man's tip. Whom will we trust on the adventure of life? Will we let go and trust God, or will we follow old patterns, traditional wisdom, habits, and bad advice in order to hang on in the various situations in which we find ourselves?

Steven Hayner, president of InterVarsity Christian Fellowship, once pointed out that "until we get to the place where we know that God is all we have, we will never know that He is all we need." When we find ourselves finally able to let go in a situation, we then see God's presence and power at work on our behalf.

Regrettably, many Christians don't experience life as a great unforgettable adventure, because they will not allow themselves to be in over their heads in the pool of life. We have a tendency to hold back and in effect block the Holy Spirit and limit His work in our lives.

Our need for control, fear of the unknown, and tendency to protect our own interests can cause us to miss what God wants to do in us. We put up protective walls and barriers designed to make our world as safe and secure as possible. Our natural inclination is to keep our control in place. Control limits our potential for a variety of wonderful outside interests that can enrich our lives and bring us great joy.

There is no adventure in a controlled existence. We were created by God to be in a relationship with Him. Apart from Him, we stand on the sidelines of life, missing out on the action, adventure, fun, and fulfillment that comes from knowing Him. To know Him and walk with Him in the adventure of faith requires that we set aside our need for control and let go. Control turns us into spectators, while surrendering control to follow Christ makes us participants in His parade.

A Fresh Perspective

To experience the adventure of faith, we need a fresh perspective: the "mind of Christ" that Paul mentions in his letter to the Philippians. The early Christians had begun to turn myopic in their faith. They were focusing on their own concerns and cares. Perhaps they were becoming spiritual "navel watchers," preoccupied with what was most immediate to them at the moment. Paul encouraged them to look "not only to your own interests, but also to the interests of others" (Phil. 2:4 NIV).

It's not that we ignore our own needs or neglect the needs of those that are close to us, but we must get a bigger picture of life in the Kingdom. Many Christians today suffer from forms of spiritual myopia. Objects and issues that loom very close are clear and immediate, but objects at a distance are blurred, confused, and unclear. We thereby fall prey to the tyranny of the urgent, moving from crisis to crisis, just trying to get through one day at a time.

Losing our perspective, it is easy to become reactors to life rather than adventuring leaders and builders of people. We tend to live existences similar to those of my pet hamsters Clem and Leroy, who lived simple lives in their cages. They ate well, slept through much of the day, then at night would get on their little wheels and run round and round, exerting much energy and effort but not going very far.

Once, when our family was relocating to a new city, we loaded the car with our suitcases, packed Clem and Leroy in the back seat, and drove off to our new home. It was an emotional time of pulling up roots, wondering how we would like the new home and job. On the way we waded through an incredible traffic jam and had one of those family fights that usually occur when everyone is stressed, sad, and tired.

Clem and Leroy never got involved. In fact, they spent most of the trip running on their little wheels, going round and round while our lives were in upheaval. From their perspective, life was unchanged. They were secure in their cages, with food, water, and fresh sawdust. But they missed the adventure of life going on all around them.

Sometimes, like those hamsters, we focus so intently on our personal comfort and the immediate tasks before us that we don't raise our eyes to see the larger world all around us. Unless we gain the focus that comes from having the mind of Christ in us, so that His priorities become our priorities, His wisdom our wisdom, and His love our love, we are doomed to spend our days running futilely around the wheel of life.

Discipleship leads us away from our comfort zones into new uncharted paths. We let go of those things that hold us back, and we look out at a big, beautiful, frightening world of adventure. Most of us only do something when we know the outcome. The result is predictability but not adventure. By lowering our expectations, we succeed, but we miss out on the new thing God wants to do in us.

While visiting a church pastored by my friend, I noticed that a missionary would be the guest speaker that evening. The bulletin had mentioned that a freewill offering would be taken for the speaker. In his office before the service, the pastor was signing a check to be given to the missionary. When I asked how he could know in advance what the offering would be, he said, "The offerings are always the same, so I can save time by writing the check now. Besides, the congregation won't give more than this amount anyway." Later I wondered whether if he had doubled the amount of the check, would the offering have doubled in size as well?

How often do we allow ourselves to be surprised by God? Have we lost the sense of wonder that comes from expecting and seeing God act in tangible ways? Discipleship can be a great adventure when we are open to being surprised along the way.

Traveling Temperaments

Because we are not all alike, the way we approach life is often a reflection of our well-developed personalities. Personality traits tend to be grouped together in certain predictable patterns that we can see in action in people's lives, whether they are following Christ on the discipleship road or taking a family vacation down the highway. Some of these types of travelers are illustrated in the following paragraphs.

Stay-at-Home Sam

This is the person who prefers order and predictability to risk and adventure. He would prefer to spend vacation time puttering around the house. "Why go anywhere?" Sams will ask. "We will only be uncomfortable, and besides there is plenty to do right here." The insightful novel *The Accidental Tourist* portrayed this type of person in all of his radiant splendor. In the book, the protagonist writes travel guides that ensure that reluctant travelers will feel that they are always right in their own homes. For Stay-at-Home Sams, life consists of maintaining structure at all costs. Their lives may be dull, but they are controlled and predictable.

Motor Home Molly

This character loves the idea of new sights and experiences but also desires the comfort and consistency of having her things around her. We've all seen those huge motor homes lumbering down the highway, bearing the earthly goods of the travelers within. It is not unusual for Motor Home Mollys to pack more than they'll ever need because they want to prepare for every emergency, never be caught without something that might come in handy, and always travel in close proximity to the comforts of home.

One summer our family borrowed a huge monster motor home and set off on vacation. We had loaded the vehicle with kitchen goods to fill the refrigerator and freezer. There was everything we'd ever need, including stereo music and a color television. The home was complete with a separate generator for those nights when we were roughing it outside a camp that had electric hookups. The master bedroom and bath were comfortable, and though we only got about five miles to the gallon in gas, it seemed that we were definitely a home on wheels.

Tour Group Gertie

This is the kind of traveler who enjoys a sense of adventure and exploration but doesn't want to actually find himself out of control. When traveling in a tour group, the itinerary is planned well in advance. The sights to be seen and the places to visit are prearranged, thus cutting down the possibility of any surprises coming along. Of course, the most important element of this style of travel is that the tour director is responsible for moving everyone along, paying the bills, and leaving appropriate tips. Thus if problems do occur, there is always someone to blame.

Fortune-and-Glory Freddy

Some people are natural-born adventurers. Like the character Indiana Jones in the movies, they roam through life with a seemingly unquenchable thirst for risk and adventure. They are the folks who will climb a mountain for no better reason than "because it is there." They like to stay flexible, keep their options open, and feel the rush of adrenalin when there is an obstacle to overcome or a mystery to be solved.

Freddy usually prefers being on the road to the confining humdrum of daily life in predictable structure. Commitments are often hard to make because, he says, "I may not be around long enough to fulfill them." There is also a tendency to be self-sufficient. This kind of traveler pretends not to need anyone, nor does he want to ever become dependent on others for anything. Accountability is virtually impossible for Freddys because that would require lasting relationships over time, and time is running out.

While each of these particular traveling temperaments has its own strengths and weaknesses, it is important to remember that none is more spiritual than any other. They are merely personality traits that have been learned and cultivated over many years. If they could be placed on a continuum between a high need for security and a high need for risk, the result looks like this graph:

High Security   High Risk

| Stay-at-Home | Motor Home | Tour Group | Fortune-and-Glory |
| Sam | Molly | Gertie | Freddy |

Once we have identified where we might place ourselves on the scale, we begin to identify our needs for security and structure, on one side, and adventure and risk, on the other. We can discover a new sense of freedom by releasing ourselves from the tyranny of reacting the same way to different opportunities.

It may be unreasonable to expect the person who prefers a more predictable existence to suddenly move to Bolivia to work in a jungle clinic, although that would be a predictable response for the more adventurous person. Likewise, it could be a frightening prospect for a person with a high need for risk to think of staying in one place over an extended period of time.

Our goal is to become open to setting aside our particular styles so that God can call us to fresh and new adventures as we follow Him in faith. Some people will learn the joy of stability and commitment as they set aside their wanderlust and discover joy in long-term commitments. Others will step out into new arenas of faith as they set aside their fear and move forward into areas that are out of their comfort zones. Wherever we find ourselves, God leads us beyond our comfortable settings and bids us follow Him in new adventure.

Different Christian communities have tended to value one personality trait over another. For example, people with high needs for security might be considered more spiritual because they are as dependable as a faithful old dog and as comfortable as an old shoe. They never challenge the system, and they rarely try anything that hasn't been proven over time. This outward solidness can look like spiritual maturity, though under the surface may be guarded individuals desperate to protect themselves from the uncertainty of life. Structure lowers anxiety, but it also lowers our capacity to embrace all of life.

Some churches have embraced the more risk-taking Christians as heroes of the faith because they are willing to go off to unknown worlds as missionaries and evangelists. Assuming that there is a spiritual value in this kind of fortune seeking, they have embraced high-risk persons, sent them to the corners of the earth, and eagerly received reports of their newest "adventures for Jesus." But it may be more helpful to encourage these persons to set aside their natural preferences in order to discover the new thing God wants to do in their life.

The Kingdom would certainly be neurotic if everyone was a Fortune-and-Glory Freddy, but it would also be dead and boring if we all were Stay-at-Home Sams. Discipleship is the process by which Jesus changes us into His image. He takes us with all of our unique and eccentric personality traits and releases us to be more than we ever imagined. Whatever type of person we may be at this point in our lives, when we say yes to Jesus and begin to follow Him, we find ourselves being changed in significant ways.

CHAPTER TWELVE

Unlocking Potential

*L*AST year I received an unusual birthday card. It read, "Birthday greetings to a confirmed pessimist. May your birthday be less rotten than it probably will be." That was meant as a good-natured joke, but I was reminded of how difficult it is to look past our current situations and past experiences to discover our potential for the future.

Too often our potential lies buried under layers of inhibitions, and those inhibitions are in part caused by the ever-present tension between our need for security and our need for excitement. Since childhood we have been alternately pursuing either safety or excitement. Now as adults we struggle with this same tension as it affects our decisions, life-styles, and priorities.

Even normal, healthy virtues can become emotional inhibitors when our lives are out of balance. For example, many of us were taught the value of thrift as a precept of life. Like the Boy Scouts, we are thrifty, kind, and good. We know the value of saving for a rainy day (although that particular phrase has dubious meaning for those of us who live in rainy Seattle, Washington). As we grow older, there are continuous reminders to save, preserve, and protect whatever limited resources we have. Deep within us lurks the message "Be safe and secure, and don't take risks."

We have all heard horror stories of people who took risks and lost everything. It happened to me. As a young man I prided myself on my skill at playing the stock market game. My pride at the time was far greater than my bank account. Foolishly, I began to think that I was invincible. Just before entering seminary, I took my portfolio of investments, teamed up with a friend, and jumped into the commodities market, hoping to make a killing.

The first week we doubled our money. The second week it doubled again. "This is too easy," I thought. I was right, it was too easy. The third week we lost everything. The fourth week I entered graduate school jobless, penniless, guilty, and a little wiser. I determined at that time that I would never take a risk again. I would only do the safe thing, with predictable and guaranteed results.

The need for safety in life is legitimate. We are not called by God to take foolish chances or be greedy or irresponsible in our finances. However, when the primary message of life is safety, or if the goal is merely to keep from losing, we may never get beyond a survival mentality to unlock our potential.

At the other extreme are those of us who have a high need for excitement and adventure. We seem to live for thrills, impulsively bounding from one experience to another, one relationship to another, seeking satisfaction without regard for the foundations necessary to support and sustain us. We flee the ordinary. We despise the mundane. Our lives look like a trail of endless midlife crises.

Our insatiable need for excitement can lead to dissatisfaction even with the good things in our lives. We are likely to develop a crisis mentality in which we allow things to go wrong just to create a situation where we must act immediately. Confirmed risk takers like to drive with the gas tank as close to empty as possible. We are exhilarated by the sense of risk and adventure as we try to find a gas station before we run out completely. In the office, an adventurer pushes deadlines back to the breaking point. Co-workers are constantly amazed when the haggard adventurer finally rushes in at the last second, delivering the project.

When the "be safe" message permeates our lives, all we can think about is protection. The preoccupation with safety clouds our thinking, freezes our relationships, blocks our dreams, and contributes to an overwhelming sense of boredom. But ardent thrill seekers are just as trapped. We find our emotions dominating our lives. When this happens, our judgment gets fuzzy, our patience dries up, and it becomes difficult to make and maintain commitments.

Both groups need to rethink how to live. It is time to allow the Lord to free us from both our need for security and our need for excitement. Inevitably, both of these drives produce inhibited living in which our potential is not fully released. We must go beyond our natural inclinations and predictable responses to experience an abundant life.

The Strange Case of Peter and Saul

I like to think of Peter as the patron saint of the neurotically impulsive. He seems so brash, daring, and freewheeling. A rugged fisherman, he left the family business to follow Jesus. At first glance he appears unreserved in his devotion to Christ, yet he fought, argued, and often misunderstood the situations in which he found himself when following the Lord.

During one argument with Jesus he was denounced as Satan by the Lord. In typical swashbuckling style, he promised undying faithfulness, only to end up lying and denying Christ in order to protect himself. While no one could fault his passionate commitment as a disciple, there was a certain instability and lack of judgment we might associate with a person who has a high need for adventure.

Saul, on the other hand, was conservative. He studied in the finest schools, kept the commandments, and faithfully executed his commitment to his religion. His credentials were impeccable. His meticulous and rigorous defense of orthodoxy led him to pursue and persecute any group that threatened to undermine the purity of the faith. Like Tevye in *Fiddler on the Roof*, Saul found security on the solid ground of his traditions.

Notice what happened when Jesus entered the lives of these two very different people. Rather than becoming merely more of what they always were, they discovered their unlimited potential for a radically different life-style.

Peter the impulsive adventurer became Peter the rock on whom Christ built His church. For most of his life he remained in and around Jerusalem. Traveling very little, he served as a pillar of orthodoxy and stability. He fought against efforts to broaden the faith beyond its Hebrew roots. He struggled against reconciling nontraditional expression of the faith with his own understanding and practice.

Saul the defensive maintainer of tradition became Paul the apostle to the world. Following his conversion, he traveled frequently, risking his life, encountering obstacles, challenging anyone who stood in the way of the gospel. Saul the religious plowhorse was transformed into an evangelistic thoroughbred who won converts and established churches wherever he went.

Like Peter and Paul, we have within us incredible potential to change the world. In order to unlock this potential, we must recognize the values and messages that are deeply ingrained in us. No longer prisoners of these characteristics, we can move beyond them and allow Christ to unleash us to live confidently even in new and unexpected roles.

The Basis for Confidence

If we have the need for security, there is assurance that Christ knows us intimately and invites us to be His friend. He stands beside us through every circumstance and every situation that arises in life.

Some of us know the torment of fear and insecurity. We long for a relationship with someone we can trust. The ultimate someone is Christ. In Him we experience peace, knowing that

He will not let us down. There is no longer a need to hold back in self-protection, for He holds nothing back from us.

We can also be confident because there is no condemnation. The only one who is in a position to ultimately judge us is now our advocate, taking our defense. We need to open the windows of our lives and allow the Lord to move through us, bringing fresh life and new hope.

It's time to admit our failures, recognize our disappointments, and release them so that our potential can be unlocked. When we cling to old resentment, failures, and pains, we in effect are saying, "I don't need help. I am in control and can take care of myself."

Another basis for confidence is that nothing can separate us from Christ's love. One of our greatest needs in life is to know where we stand, to know that we are loved. We need assurance that those who matter most to us will be there when we need them.

Through a divorce recovery program, I met a little boy whose parents were divorcing. The father had moved out unexpectedly, and the mother had sole custody of the child. He said that his biggest fear was that someday he would do something wrong and his mother would leave, just like dad left; "the worst part is that I'm afraid I won't even know what I did to make her go away."

Many of us carry inside the fear that something will happen that will cause those who matter the most to us, who are most significant, maybe even God Himself, to give up on us and walk out of our lives forever. The promise of Christ is "I will never leave you." There are no barriers or walls we can erect that are big enough to keep out His love for us.

Steps for Unlocking Potential

Seek Security Where It Can Be Found

Americans are notorious for applying good solutions to the
wrong problems. We are ingenious at identifying problems, but
we seem helpless to resolve them. There is nothing inherently
wrong with desiring safety and security, or with wanting excitement in life. But no matter how secure we want to be, a bigger
sword, thicker and higher walls, a fuller table, more toys will not
bring the results we crave. Only the peace of knowing to whom
we belong can satisfy that longing. He brings assurance in the
midst of an uncertain world.

Don't Settle for Mere Problem Solving

There is more to life than winning or losing. Too often we settle
for being the best we can be on our own strength. Bookstores
are filled with self-help literature, pop psychologists abound,
magazines promote the latest fads and self-fulfillment techniques.
All of these resources and more stand ready to give us helpful
bits of advice on becoming overcomers of setbacks, obstacles,
pain, suffering, or whatever else ails us. But this is only living
within our means. Overcoming suffering and solving problems,
while important, only bring us up to zero on the scale of life's
potential. We need Christ to take us beyond that.

Try Something That Is Beyond Your Abilities

Perhaps one of the reasons we don't see more miracles in our
world today is that we usually only attempt things we know can
be accomplished successfully. We don't need miracles any more.
Our thinking has grown so small that we are overwhelmed by
big issues. Rather than take risks, we seek guarantees. Unfortunately, the only guarantee we are apt to find is the assurance of
becoming small-minded people in a small-minded world.

See Pain as God's Attention Getter

When you find yourself in a frustrating, painful situation, it is time to ask God at least two questions: "Lord, what do You want to have happen in me as a result of this pain?" and "Lord, what do You want me to do?" These questions can help us to look creatively at our lives. They move us away from the self-pitying "Why?" questions and allow us to put the focus where it belongs, on our relationship with Christ.

Dan was a bright and popular student at Seattle Pacific University. He had everything going for him, and he seemed to excel in every area. Dan married Connie, his high school sweetheart, and went on to graduate from law school in southern California. His life was getting better and better. With the birth of a beautiful daughter, passing the bar exam and landing a job with a prominent law firm, Dan could not have been happier as he drove home from work.

Before reaching home that night, Dan's car was struck from behind, leaving him paralyzed from the neck down. His life was never the same. He became an outspoken advocate for the rights of physically impaired persons and contributed countless hours to mission and relief agencies.

Dan had a recurring problem with headaches. It was frustrating that the only part of his body that had any feeling was prone to headaches. When the usual home remedies did not stop the pain, he called his doctor, who immediately brought him into the hospital for tests. The source of the pain was discovered and taken care of.

Since that experience, he knows that a headache is a signal that something is wrong somewhere in his body, so he quickly gets to the hospital. It is a referred pain that indicates a breakdown somewhere—a broken arm, internal bleeding, a heart attack. The signal is in his head.

It is possible that we, like Dan, experience referred pain in our lives. We are uncertain of its cause and are not able to accurately diagnose the specific need. We need to use that pain as an opportunity to stop and assess our situation, allowing God to get our attention and lead us into new areas of healing and growth.

Allow Problems to Be a Catalyst for Ministry

Some of the most effective ministries I know of have grown out of the seedbed of personal pain and suffering. Several years ago, a few people in our church were sharing with one another the hurt they felt over their divorce experiences. Out of that exchange came a divorce recovery ministry that has helped thousands of men, women, and children heal from the pain of broken marriages. Similar programs have been developed for a variety of human situations.

We have a choice: We can choose to let God use our pain, or we can let our pain abuse us. I doubt if we will ever get pain free in this life. But we do have the power to live in spite of our hurt. We can even turn life's worst into a tool for healing and helping others.

Don't Miss the Good as You Go

We don't have to be like Eeyore the negative donkey in A. A. Milne's *Winnie the Pooh*. Nevertheless, the tendency is to keep our heads down while we focus on the many problems before us. After all, difficulties usually seem much more immediate than their solutions.

Recently in a small group in which I was participating, we were asked to share reflections of the past year. I started to give my little laundry list of difficulties I had faced when I suddenly realized that this had been the best year of my life, and I had missed it! I had missed out on the joy and happiness of the best year of my life, because I had kept my head down each day, unable to look up and enjoy the miracles that God was doing all around me, in me, through me, and even in spite of me. I had been so worried about what wasn't happening, or what needed to happen, or what problem might happen that I hadn't enjoyed the year!

Since then, I have decided not to miss any more years. They may be good, they may be bad, but I am going to enjoy them regardless. I am determined not to miss the good as I go.

The tension between our need for safety and our need for excitement may never be resolved. But Jesus Christ meets both of these needs. He leads us into a whole new dimension of living. He unlocks our potential, as we come face to face with Him and discover the grace that moves us beyond our circumstances, secure in His love, bolstered by His power, and set free in ministry. The potential is unlimited.

PART·IV

A Colorful
Life-style

CHAPTER THIRTEEN

Unbound Passion

S_{OME} people rise above mediocrity and the mundane. They tackle seemingly overwhelming obstacles and are tireless in their efforts to experience life at its fullest. Michael Meyer, writing in *The Alexander Complex*, says, "What distinguishes the empire builders from others is their passion. They devote their lives to an idea that in time becomes an ideal. More important, they inspire others to buy into their dream. All are out in one way or other, to change the world."

"Only passions, great passions, can elevate the soul to great things," said French author Diderot. Passion, like the wind, is sometimes difficult to describe in its absence but is very evident when it is present. Followers of Christ have good reason to be the most passionate people on earth; after all, we are loved and accepted by God. We are forgiven and healed through Christ's work on the cross. We are empowered and unleashed in ministry by the Holy Spirit.

The birth of the church in Acts is an account of men and women caught by the burning passion of their conviction, discovering how to set the world right as they lived out the implications of their faith. Now, after two thousand years of experience, we are struggling to rediscover the unbound passion that those first disciples experienced. Where did the passion go? This is not merely a historical issue for us. It is a critical need in our lives.

Threats to Passion

If we are to rekindle the flames of passionate living, it is important to recognize what cools passion and diminishes our enthusiasm. Three threats to passionate living are institutionalism, predictability, and indifference.

Institutionalism

We live in the tension between the organic and the organization. What begins with life and vitality soon becomes organized, structured, and dead. Adventure and risk soon give way to procedures and policies, until the fun is squeezed from life. The institutionalization of a relationship begins to plant the seeds of deadness and undermines its passion. "Marriage is a great institution, but I'm not ready for an institution," Mae West said.

The church is a classic example of organization gone wrong. What began with the wind and fire of the Spirit has become a bloated structure that reels under the oppressive weight of its own dysfunctional complexity. "The Spirit builds the house," Emerson observed, "and then the house confines the Spirit."

One of the reasons that passion dies in institutions is that the concern of an institution must be primarily its own survival. Thus goals are determined according to survivalist strategies rather than strategies seeking fresh new ways to relate and function. Safety is important from an institutional mind-set. Risk taking is minimized, and conformity is rewarded.

Large corporations, pressured by the growth of innovative entrepreneurial companies, are beginning to effect changes in their organizations to allow for more flexibility and creativity. The idea of encouraging creativity within the system has fostered the new word "intrapreneuring," which describes creative idea development that is nurtured within an institution. It is seen as a fresh hope for encumbered corporations.

In the church, denominations are being forced to change their perspectives in an effort to reverse plummeting membership and financial bases. New church development, almost nonexistent in mainline churches since the 1950s, is resurging as one way to counter this decline. Innovations in worship and congregational life are being explored in an effort to gain a foothold in the lives of the baby boom generation.

Years of growing discontent about marriage have led to fear and reservation about entering into the institution of marriage. Most of us have our favorite snide quotation about marriage. I like Cher's observation: "The trouble with some women is that they get all excited about nothing—and then they marry him." H. L. Mencken reminds us that "men have a much better time of it than women; for one thing they marry later; for another thing they die earlier."

Institutions are a fact of life. They will probably always be with us, so it does no good to merely lament their presence. We can, however, intentionally strive to infuse our lives with passion even in the context of our institutions. We can do this by gaining a fresh perspective that is free from the tyranny of a survival mentality.

Predictability

Playing the part of a prep school literature teacher in the film *Dead Poets' Society*, Robin Williams leaps onto his desk and challenges the class to look at life from a different perspective as they read their poetry. Sometimes we have to do unusual things to break out of stifling cycles of predictability.

A vital, passionate relationship becomes ordinary, safe, and guarded the longer we are in it. One of the things contributing to this deadness is that we begin to treat each other with predictability. Surprises begin to diminish, and habits are developed in the relationship. Assuming that we know how another person will respond, we cease to relate to him or her with either interest or immediacy. We begin to think, mistakenly, "I know what she would say, so I don't need to ask her opinion."

Jesus' style of ministry was very unpredictable. Both His teaching and His behavior continually kept people off balance. When the rich young ruler greeted Him by saying, "Good Master," Jesus retorted that he should "call no man good." At the news of His friend's fatal illness, Jesus dallied and procrastinated until Lazarus died, much to the chagrin of the grieving family. Yet when He was hurrying along His way, pressed for time, He stopped to heal a woman who reached out to touch His clothing as He rushed by.

Teaching life lessons by parable was confusing to many of His disciples. "To help men see, I throw dust in their eyes," said James Joyce. I'm sure that there were times that Jesus' followers, hearing Him teach, felt as if dust had been blown into their eyes. Yet the very unpredictability of His lessons and behavior enabled some people to hear the truth in fresh and life-changing ways.

Indifference

The opposite of love is not hate; it is indifference. Perhaps nothing cools passion quite as effectively as the words "I don't care." In the book of Revelation, (RSV), God says, "Would that you were cold or hot. So because you are lukewarm, I will spew you out of my mouth." Relationships can tolerate and even intensify with struggle and tension. However, the passivity that comes from indifference is a destroyer of intimacy, an underminer of relationships.

The Bible is filled with accounts of people who would not settle for passive indifference toward God. King David, who was called "a man after God's own heart" (Acts 13:22), is an example of someone who was passionate in his commitment to God. In spite of being both a hero and a scoundrel, he refused to live indifferently.

We are called to live in such a way that we never settle for the immobilizing attitude of indifference. "If you aren't fired with enthusiasm, you will be fired, with enthusiasm," Vince

Lombardi instructed his teams. Jesus advised His disciples that He did not come to bring peace but a sword. He would turn family members against one another as they were confronted with His claims on their lives. Following Jesus requires passion; we dare not settle for apathetic indifference.

Passion Builders

In order to cultivate a healthy passion in our lives, we need a clear sense of identity, ability to focus on the needs of others, autonomy to act according to our principles, and freedom to grow and change.

Sense of Identity

Passion grows when we have a clear sense of personal identity that is acknowledged and reinforced by significant people in our lives. If we sense that we are being scrutinized or evaluated, or that we are not meeting with approval, then we become insecure and unsure of the relationship. If we feel judged or lack a clear sense of our strengths, weaknesses, and standing with God, it may be difficult to throw ourselves into a relationship unreservedly.

In my early years I had a reputation for being the class clown. I was the person who always had a witty comment to make others laugh. Deep inside I knew that there was a serious and sensitive person lurking behind the funny exterior, but other people only related to me on the superficial level.

When I first met the woman I would eventually marry, there was something very different about the way she related to me. She was one of the first people I knew that I didn't feel like I had to entertain. I didn't have to carry the conversation or do something wild and funny to impress her. It was freeing to be with someone who didn't expect me to be the clown. There was something in the way she looked at me that reinforced an identity that I knew was inside of me but wasn't being demonstrated in my other relationships.

Identity is more than just who we are inside. It also involves our need to be *recognized* for who we are. It is a two-part issue: One part is how we see ourselves; the other part is how we are perceived. For example, we may be responsible, competent people given great respect at the office, but at home be treated like idiots. We need to be able to look into other people's eyes and feel good about ourselves.

Unfortunately there are people in all of our lives who will always see us in a negative light. No matter how we grow and change, their perception remains the same. I remember my high school German teacher, who saw me as loser. Through little barbs, comments, and remarks, he communicated that I was not going to amount to anything in life. Years later, I ran into him outside the graduate offices at the university. He was stunned to see that I was apparently doing well in my life. As we talked briefly, I realized that in his mind I would always remain "the loser kid."

We need others who will look beyond our obvious strengths and weaknesses to see the vast potential below the surface. We give one another a great gift when we begin to call forth qualities and characteristics that may have lain dormant all of our lives. In the process we blossom into confident, passionate people.

Ability to Focus on Needs

Passionate living comes from engagement, involvement, looking below the surface to pick up on the real needs of people. In order to focus on needs, we must let go of our tendency to generalize and stereotype people, in order to see them as unique individuals.

In Acts 4 we find Peter and John caught up in their usual routine, going to church like they always did. They started to pass by a man who was begging in the spot where he had sat for many years. People had probably walked by so many times that they never really saw him anymore.

Peter and John could have passed by, relating to him predictably, in a nonpassionate way. But this day was different. Suddenly they began to treat him differently than they had on previous days. "Peter looked straight at the man and said, 'Look at us'."

They shared briefly, then Peter took him by the hand and lifted him to his feet, as the healing power of God restored the man's body. The simple act of tuning in to the man's life and needs, coupled with faith in the risen Christ, began a series of miracles that resulted in an unleashing of the transforming Spirit of God.

Have you ever noticed that in our relationships we sometimes get to the point where we don't really look at one another anymore. Perhaps we need to stop and say, "Look at me, I'm a real person and I need you." Then we can start to give one another full attention.

In our marriages it can be easy to get out of touch. We settle for talking about circumstances, issues, and current problems, but we don't tune in to the other person and focus on their feelings, thoughts, and needs. To counter this, my wife and I use a simple but helpful exercise. Timing ourselves with a watch, we each take fifteen minutes to tell what we are feeling, while the other person sits quietly. Then we switch, and the other person gets to share feelings for fifteen minutes. While it only takes a half-hour time commitment, it helps us to get in touch with our feelings and really listen to each other without interrupting. At the end of the time we discover that we don't feel so distracted or out of touch. Instead, we feel listened to, valued, and loved.

Passion can be restored in relationships, if we tune in and listen to the needs of the other person. Getting below the surface is a two-way street. We listen to the other, and we give of ourselves. In the honesty of that exchange, communication is deepened, and love can be released.

Autonomy to Act

Autonomy involves power to serve, care, and function according to our purposes. It is the power to make a difference. Passion grows when we have freedom to make decisions and implement our plans. When we feel powerless to make a difference, our passion diminishes. But if we encourage one another to dream of new ways to serve, passion is released. Sometimes the simplest effort can produce the greatest results. All it takes is for men and women of faith to look with courage past the glaringly apparent obstacles.

Most of us hold back because we feel unqualified or ill-prepared. We don't want to appear foolish, nor do we want to fail. The greatest failure of all, though, is not to have tried. History is filled with great failures. Many of them now seem funny because of their stupidity. But success most often comes on the heels of numerous failures and false starts. Passion grows best in an atmosphere where we are granted the freedom to fail as well as to succeed.

My church was invigorated by the simple act of gathering the congregation together in small dessert groups where we could share with one another a dream for ministry. The dreams didn't have to be practical or workable. We didn't even need to have a strategy for implementation. Hundreds of people met in groups and talked about their dreams. Some people started to share by saying, "This is probably silly, but . . ." Others said, "I know this won't work, but . . ."

There is power in sharing your dream, whatever it is. To be carriers of the Spirit means that we will be dreamers. If we will tap into the wealth of creativity and loving concern that lies bubbling just below the surface, we will experience a fresh burst of passion as we are mobilized in ministry.

"I was taught as a little girl to share my food," remembers Gloria. "I wanted to do something for those less fortunate than me, but thought, what could one person do? I talked about it with some friends, and soon we began making sandwiches in our kitchen. We take them downtown and help feed homeless people in the shelters. We make as many as 800 sandwiches at a time, and we are having great fun doing it!" Who could imagine a trio of beautiful retired ladies, lashing out at hunger in their city and having fun in the process?

God's Desperados

Most of us like the passion and intrigue associated with being part of a secret order. It can be fun to secretly care for people so that they don't know whom to thank. A band of secret ministers emerged from the singles ministry at my church a few years ago. No one knows who they are, but they have captured the imagination of the whole congregation with their antics.

They have been known to repair cars while the unemployed owner is at a meeting in the church. Everything from home repairs to yard work for shut-ins has been occurring mysteriously because of the Desperados. One single parent in financial distress reported that her daughter ran to inform her that strange men were at the door. Apprehensively, she opened the door and greeted two men wearing bandana scarves over their faces, who delivered a seemingly endless stream of groceries and household supplies. The children were so excited by the treasure trove of goodies that they wanted to sleep in the living room with all the groceries. Her young son, who had cerebral palsy, climbed up on the largest watermelon he had ever seen and rode it like a horse. As the two strangers turned to leave, they waved and called out, "Adios!" God's desperados had struck again.

Last week I received a letter from an elderly lady in the church. "I'm writing to you because I don't know who to thank. My husband has been very ill with heart trouble, and I am not very strong. This winter our wood supply had run out, and we had no other way to heat our house. I didn't know what to do. Some men, whom I didn't know, came to our house and asked if they could help. Before I knew it they had cut and stacked enough firewood to last all year. I'm sending a picture that I took of them at work; in case you recognize them, please thank them for me and my husband." God's desperados had struck again.

Who are God's desperados? Anyone who wants to look at the needs around us and do something about them. We can even be desperados for Jesus at work, secretly praying for the person in the next office, or looking for opportunities to encourage, bless, and help a person who is having a difficult time. It requires no organization, no budget, and no administration. Like the ad for Nike shoes says, you, "just do it!"

Freedom to Grow

Passion is rekindled where we experience the freedom to grow and change. It is exciting to visit with couples years after their weddings. Bill and Sarah, a couple that I had married many years ago, invited me to their home. They confided a discovery that they both thought might be a problem in their marriage. "He just isn't the same man I married back then," Sarah commented. "He has changed in so many ways, he is hardly the same person."

"You think I'm different," Bill retorted. "What about you? You are continually changing. I sometimes feel tired just trying to keep up with you." They were experiencing the effects of having a healthy relationship in our fast-paced world. We live in a time when change is the norm, and if we don't grow together, we will find ourselves growing apart.

Rather than fearing change or resisting it, we can embrace change as a friend. It helps us to gain new fresh approaches to problems. It keeps us from stagnating. Most of all, it prods us toward new challenges and adventures.

Even though I believe change and growth are positive and necessary parts of my life, I don't particularly like change. I don't mind when others need to grow, but when it is my turn, I tend to dig in and become resistant and a bit anxious. Perhaps I am resistant because change and growth disrupt my comfortable, controlled world. Even if I'm not completely happy with the way things are, I would rather not upset everything with something new or different. Isn't it ironic that many of us prefer the bad that we know to the possible good that we don't know?

Change can be disruptive and difficult. It can also stimulate us to grow in fresh ways. We may choose to resist change, but when we let go of the familiar to take hold of the new, there is a sense of passion and excitement that lets us know we are alive.

I sometimes picture the church hunkered down in a corner hoping that life will not ask too much of her or change her too drastically. Part of experiencing unbound passion is the discovery of courage to move beyond reacting to circumstances. Instead we become active in expressing our faith.

No longer must we sit back and wait for changes to happen to us. We are initiators of change. Gone is the feeling of powerlessness or the inability to make a difference. If anyone can make life better, it is "Christ in you, the hope of glory." Unbound passion is not always comfortable, nor is it an easy way to live. But it sure beats the alternative of dull spiritual impotence.

CHAPTER FOURTEEN

Unbridled Confidence

*I*T'S hard to be confident in an uncertain world. Change is a constant companion in our fast-paced lives. It seems to be increasingly difficult to experience true, unbridled confidence. Davy Crockett's motto was "Be always sure you are right, then go ahead." But how can we be always sure that we are right? That kind of confidence evades us. There are so many changes happening all around, it is increasingly difficult to be sure about anything.

Governments change. Countries that were our mortal enemies are now our friends and allies. The "evil empire" of the Cold War becomes our partner in goodwill. Eastern Europe hurtles toward democracy and unity in unexpected ways. Political climates change, putting pressure on governments to realign and shift priorities. We find ourselves unable to respond and adjust quickly to the changes in our world.

Economies change. No longer agricultural or industrial in our economic focus, we are becoming an information society. Information brings power, and power brings money. Our world is drawing closer together because of the instant accessibility of communication and information.

Relationships are changing. The rules for relationships are constantly being rewritten. It can be confusing to enter relationships not knowing the expectations and pitfalls that await the unsuspecting. Sexual roles have changed significantly in the last decades. First Lady Barbara Bush was initially rejected as a commencement speaker at Wellesley College because she had chosen to be a wife and mother rather than to pursue a career. Although she went ahead and spoke despite the protests, this signal of change in attitude resonated throughout the country.

Years ago Bob Dylan's anthem "The Times They Are A-Changing" foretold our current experiences in which he warned parents that a new generation was evolving. When that was first sung, it was the defiant challenge of a young generation. Now it is an uncertain warning to that same generation. They are now themselves mothers and fathers, who seem less self-confident than they did twenty-some years ago.

Is it any wonder that we lack stability and confidence? My grandmother Nell has lived in the same white house in Los Angeles for most of her ninety-three years. Her children grew up in that house, as did her grandchildren. Now great-grandchildren come to visit, exploring the nooks and gardens that have intrigued four generations.

I can remember my grandparents having only one car since the 1960s. It was a beige Chevy Impala that lasted until they stopped driving. Their vacations were usually spent camping and fishing in Montana. They had the innate ability to locate the same campsite each year, where they would spend the summers.

I appreciate the stability my grandparents represented. But my experience wasn't the same. The first fifteen years of my marriage, we lived in seventeen homes. I owned nineteen cars, most of which didn't run very well. I changed jobs thirteen times. Furthermore, we never vacationed in the same place twice. Although I don't enjoy change, I seem to do it quite often.

Sometimes we think that if we just knew what was ahead in the future, we could live with greater confidence. There are times when we wish we could read God's mind and know what He wants us to do. The problem is that we usually discern God's will only in hindsight. We'll probably never know it in advance.

Throughout the ages people have sought the help of seers and psychics to help them discern the future. The Reuters news agency reported on the failure of professional psychics who are featured regularly in the supermarket tabloids. In 1989 alone they failed to foresee the collapse of the Berlin wall, the San Francisco earthquake, the political unrest in China, or the U.S. invasion of Panama.

One psychic predicted in the *National Examiner* that Panamanian dictator Manuel Noriega would step down and move to New York, where he would seek to become a photographer's model for a pineapple juice distributor. Another prediction that failed to materialize was that a French psychic would "astound the world with a mind-transfer demonstration that produces a talking cat." Tragedy would follow when the fleeing feline would be struck dead by a bus, leaving the psychic stuck as a cat.

Our desire to know the future or to make the right choice, causes us to long for guidance. We look for big events that may affect or alter our lives. However, very few of our most significant experiences happen in the big moments of our lives. Rather, our lives tend to be shaped by the little things, the small commitments, actions, and events that sneak up on us. We usually don't recognize their significance at the time, but in hindsight we realize their importance.

Our desire to "know God's will" can be linked to a desire to predict and control the future. Much energy and time is spent speculating and sometimes worrying about the possibilities of the future. But we never really know what is ahead for us. That is why we must exercise faith, believing that God will be present in an uncertain future.

There are times I identify with Charlie Brown in the "Peanuts" cartoon. Lucy promises to hold the football so that he can kick it. Charlie knows that she can't be trusted because experience has shown him that at the last moment she will yank the ball away, leaving him flat on his back, filled with frustration. But Lucy is insistent that she can be trusted this time, so Charlie runs hard and kicks with all his might, only to have the ball pulled away one more time.

Confidence comes not from our ability to maintain a grip on the future but from operating on the assumption that there is One who does know the future and gives credence to our hopes. The Lord promises to be with us in times of joy and pain. Our tendency is to hold back because we have been let down by others so many times. Confidence in God is not merely a blind leap of faith, however. It can be built over a period of time. Like any honest relationship, it is not cultivated instantaneously, nor is it always on our terms. It is real, however, and will result in unbridled confidence if we will give it a chance.

Builders of Confidence

Confidence is built when we *know each other intimately*.

The Psalmist, writing in the Old Testament, describes how God knows us before we are even born. While our lives may appear to be a dark mystery to ourselves and the people around us, they are not a mystery to God. He understands the swirl of our hopes, fears, and dreams. He understands our mixed motives and odd combinations of strengths and weaknesses. While we may try to hide parts of ourselves from others and even live in denial with ourselves, we are not hidden from God.

I can still remember my infant son playing peek-a-boo in the evening. He would focus his attention on me, then quickly cover his eyes. While his eyes were covered, he thought that I couldn't see him. In effect, he had become invisible in his own mind, because he couldn't see through the palms of his tiny hands.

How often do we assume that just because we have spiritual or relational blinders over our eyes, no one can see us? From God's perspective we are in plain view, but from our viewpoint we are isolated and alone. It is possible to feel all alone, thinking that we alone are going through whatever struggles and difficulties we are experiencing.

Sometimes we assume that no one else is feeling the emotions that well up inside us. Surely no one can understand our fears and doubts. It is important to remember that God is not surprised. He already knows us. He loves us for who we are and for whom we might become by His loving presence in our lives.

In Romans 8, Paul reminds us that we often don't know how to pray or what to pray about. Yet God knows our situations and the longings of our hearts and is already acting on our behalf before we verbalize our prayers.

A second builder of confidence is our *past experience*. My wife keeps prayer journals in which she records her prayer requests, along with the date and manner in which God answered the prayer. Over the years she has filled dozens of books with specific, tangible, and sometimes miraculous accounts of answered prayer. These notebooks have become a physical reminder of God's past faithfulness. But we aren't limited to writing in journals in order to remember. Some of us are more verbal; we can talk about what God has done. Share the stories of answered prayer whenever you get a chance. Like the ancient Hebrews, we can start our own oral tradition.

It makes it easier to trust Him for the current situations when we remember His faithfulness in the past. Ken Medema encourages people to tell their story in songs. George Mueller entitled his journal *50,000 Answers to Prayer*. In it he demonstrated the confidence that comes from recognizing God's faithfulness in the past. He understood that if we don't write down God's acts on our behalf, in time the memory will fade, and we will once again question whether or not God cares for us. Whether you write, talk, sing, or paint pictures, it is important to express what God is doing in your life.

A third builder of confidence is developing *character* within ourselves and recognizing character in the other person. Character is demonstrated over the long journey. It begins with a small act and grows into a mark of identity. "Sow an act and you reap a habit. Sow a habit and you reap a character. Sow a character and you reap a destiny," observed Charles Reade in the 1800s.

When we find our beliefs and behaviors merging, we are on the road to building character. It is particularly evident when we struggle in difficult and frustrating times. The Psalmist could write, "Though I walk through the valley of the shadow of death, I will fear no evil: for thou art with me" (KJV). When life's worst is not enough to separate us from the consistent love and presence of God, we acquire a durable confidence for the unexpected and uncontrollable things that lie ahead.

Unfortunately, we are slow to discover God's authentic character, as revealed in Scripture. We are, however, quick to project our own insecurities and fears onto Him. For instance, it can be painful for a person who grew up in an abusive home to picture God as a loving parent. Yet breaking free of preconceived images is a necessary step toward building a confident relationship with the living Lord.

When my friend Jimmy Johnson was challenged by someone who said she didn't believe in God, Jimmy responded by saying, "Tell me about this God you don't believe in—I probably don't believe in him either." This response recognized that we all have inadequate conceptions of God that don't line up with His own self-revelation in the Bible and in the person of Jesus Christ.

It is no wonder that we feel so insecure when it comes to trusting God with our lives. Getting to know Him and allowing Him to know us breaks down those walls of defensiveness and frees us to walk in confidence because we know His character and we are being molded into His image. God has something special in mind for you and me. Paul reminds us that we are predestined to be conformed to the image of Christ. This is the intent of God when He envisions our lives as whole people. Our maturing process becomes the steps that lead us to realize God's dream for us. We may not know the particular angles and quirks of the future, but we do know the goal to which we move—Christlikeness.

The fourth builder of confidence is *openness of communication*. Most of us recognize the discomfort of sensing that someone is not being completely open with us. When we feel that information is being withheld or facts are being distorted, our confidence in the person is weakened. Yet when people are vulnerable and share candidly from their perspective, we are willing to trust without reservation.

In spite of this observation, it seems increasingly difficult for people to communicate openly and honestly. Abraham Lincoln remarked, "I am a firm believer in the people. If given the truth, they can be depended upon to meet any national crisis. The great point is to bring them the real facts."

Our guarded attitudes leave us distorting facts, withholding the truth, and telling people what we think they want to hear rather than what is true. This is unfortunately occurring in most areas of life. Whether it is in our family, politics, church, or education, we seem to have lost the willingness or capability for open communication.

When I was involved in a building program for my church, I found it very difficult to communicate the current financial picture to the congregation. Members of the building committee, contractors, architects, and well-meaning church leaders could not agree on the facts. All we needed were figures that were both true and understandable. One man came with a set of figures that were simple, straightforward, and easy to understand, but they were not true. He had merely made them up, without regard for accuracy. Another person had notebooks of detailed information. His facts were accurate, his notes were copious, and his details unending. His figures were absolutely true, but when he was finished explaining, no one understood what he was talking about.

Is it any wonder we are experiencing a lack of confidence in one another? While it is easy to target leaders in industry, government, and the church as the culprits, the case could be made that the problem belongs to every one of us. Confidence erodes when communication is not true and clear. I am coming to appreciate Tom Lehrer's observation, "I wish people who have trouble communicating would just shut up."

Upon his release from prison, South African activist Nelson Mandela embarked on a world tour to speak out against apartheid and answer critics of the organization he represented. It was obvious that he was not a man groomed for public posturing. His remarks were often candid, sometimes shocking, and obviously unrehearsed. It was apparent that part of his appeal was the very fact that he seemed indifferent to the opinions of his audience. Whether or not he was liked, or whether folks approved of his tactics, he was speaking the truth as he saw it, with great clarity.

The Comparison Trap

When we are faced with obstacles that appear overwhelming, it is a natural response to pull back. Our perceptions of ourselves can be distorted. It is tempting at times like that to fall into the mind trap of comparing ourselves with others, thus reinforcing the belief that we are not adequate.

When the people of Israel came up to the promised land, their spies reported horrifying accounts of the lands and people that lay ahead. "There were giants in the land. We looked like grasshoppers in our own eyes and that is what we seemed like to them" (Numbers 13:33).

When I am faced with a difficult challenge or am about to enter uncharted waters, it is a natural response for me to compare myself with those around me, and I too begin to see myself as a grasshopper. I am acutely aware of all of my real and imagined inadequacies, so it is easy to lose confidence when I am afraid or feeling threatened.

My friend and colleague Tim Snow recalls the time he was giving swimming lessons to a group of preschool children. All of the kids had jumped into the pool except one little toddler, who stood on the edge of the pool with large fear-filled eyes. Tim used all of his skill and charm to try to coax the little girl into the water, but nothing seemed to work. Finally with her eyes brimming with tears, she said, "I guess I'm not as big as I look."

None of us are as big or as small as we look. Nor do we have to be limited by the opinions of others, self-perceptions, or obstacles (real or imagined) in our way. Secure confidence is ours when we discover that we are loved and accepted unreservedly by God. I used to have a poster in my office as a daily reminder of the source of confidence for each one of us: "There is nothing you can do to get God to love you one bit more than He does right now. There is also nothing you can do to get Him to love you one bit less than He does right now."

CHAPTER FIFTEEN

Uncompromising Conviction

*T*HE summer sun felt a little too hot as I sat at the traffic light with the top down on my convertible. Glancing at the station wagon in front of me, I could barely make out the words of the faded bumper sticker. "If you don't stand for something," it read, "you'll fall for anything."

As the light turned green and we drove on, I wondered about the things I stood for. Our convictions become a mirror of the values and priorities in our lives. "Choose your battles wisely," a friend warned me. "It isn't possible to fight for everything." To stand with uncompromising conviction is a true act of faith.

It has been sarcastically said that "a conviction is that commendable quality in ourselves which we call bullheadedness in others." On the positive side, Bishop Francis Kelly observed, "Convictions are the mainsprings of action, the driving powers of life."

Followers of Christ have long been women and men of uncompromising conviction. We are people of faith and vision, in a world that longs for both of those rare commodities. Our conviction is not a vague intellectual concept. Rather, it is rooted in our own experience of the power of God in our everyday lives.

Paul writes, "I know in whom I have believed. And I am convinced that He is able." We too can live out the implications of firm convictions based not on our own abilities or achievements but on the character and work of God on our behalf.

Convictions always lead to action. James reminds us that "faith without works is dead." Our beliefs will weaken and fade if they don't find tangible expression. None of us feels completely confident as we live out our faith. The possibility of failure is very real. Sometimes success can create even more problems than we think we can handle. Success and failure are not determiners of our ministry.

In Mark 6, Jesus is amazed. He has been a washout, as far as ministry goes. People were not only unimpressed as He moved through His home region, they were offended by Him and indignant that this upstart from the village would be so presumptuous. Jesus found Himself unable to do any miracles in their midst. Although no doubt frustrated in His attempts to minister, the Lord does a surprising thing—He gives the ministry away as He empowers and sends out the disciples, two by two.

I think that the church may have been born that day. Jesus found Himself unable to minister because of the people's unbelief, and rather than giving up in righteous resignation, He called the disciples together, gave them authority, and sent them out into neighboring villages to do the ministry themselves.

Imagine the disciples' hesitation when they were given this assignment. Their Master was an apparent failure; He couldn't do anything, and no one listened to Him, so what chance did they have? Suddenly their convictions were being put to the test.

To make matters worse, Jesus instructed them to unpack their bags and leave behind the very necessities that would make their journey bearable. "Take nothing for your journey except a staff, no bread, no bag, no money in your belts. Wear sandals but not an extra tunic."

Perhaps what we choose to leave behind on a journey is more important than what we decide to take with us. Maybe we should sit down and make a list, when packing our bags, of all the things we are *not* going to take.

Baggage We Carry

We are held back by many different kinds of baggage. One of our burdens is the baggage of self-reliance and personal security. Our need to be ready for any emergency causes us to overprepare. We may not have extra tunics or moneybelts, but we do have a lot of excess emotional baggage, family baggage, religious baggage, that hinders us from moving out as Christ directs us.

We sometimes cling to memories of the past, successes or failures, or ideas about the way things were, are, or should be in the future. Sometimes we are burdened by the baggage of hopes and fears about what might be ahead—or what might not be ahead for us.

When I get a little insecure, I want to have things or people in my life that I can lean on for security and comfort. Like Linus in the "Peanuts" cartoon, we've all got our security blankets to bolster our courage. They take a little different shape for each of us, but they are there nonetheless. As long as there are lesser things for us to place our trust upon, we will tend to resist truly trusting Jesus Christ.

Why does Jesus insist on our setting aside these apparently harmless confidence builders? Could it be that He wanted there to be no doubt as to the reason for our surprising success? As long as you carry everything you will ever need, you will never need Him. Christ's invitation is to let Him provide for you, be your covering and defense while you journey.

The baggage of self-reliance can hold us back, keeping us from experiencing God's miracles each day. Perhaps we don't see Him at work because we have already taken care to meet our own needs. Striving to stay in control, we unwittingly put ourselves in a position where we don't have to trust God.

While discussing some of the cultural changes taking place in our country, a friend observed, "In the sixties, we studied sociology because we wanted to change our world. Then in the seventies we studied psychology, so that we could change ourselves. In the eighties we studied business management so that we could secure our future." Now, in the nineties, personal comfort and security have become the standards by which decisions are made, goals are set, and priorities are lived out. This is the antithesis of living by faith.

Remember the old phrase "the generation gap"? A few years ago the younger generation revolted against the older generation. They rejected their values, standards, and life-styles, saying, "We are going to do it differently!" Today we don't hear about a generation gap. Our kids are every bit as comfort seeking and security conscious as we are.

Our convictions are stronger than the opinions and approval of others. Perhaps nothing erodes our confidence and blurs our vision as much as the baggage of trying to please others. We judge our success or failure by other people's responses. Naturally, we want to be liked and appreciated by those around us. So we carry the baggage of "playing for the crowd."

We need to know that our worth and loveability are unrelated to others' approval or disapproval. No matter how hard we try, some will respond, and others will be turned off. Jesus understood this and gave to His disciples very helpful advice: "If any place will not welcome you or listen to you, shake the dust off your feet when you leave, as a testimony against them" (Matt. 10:14 NIV).

Lloyd Ogilvie calls this our "Sacrament for Failure." Just as the Bread and Cup bind us together in the sacrament of Communion, and the poured water of Baptism ushers us into the covenant community, so too does this ritual free us forever of the burden of failure, missed opportunity, inadequacy, or ineffectiveness.

Jesus' words gave the first disciples freedom from the tyranny of having to succeed or trying to please others. They became free to trust God and live out their faith regardless of the responses of others.

How we need this sacrament today. It is so easy to fall prey to the "please me" game. We search one another's eyes seeking clues to let us know whether or not we are loveable. Unfortunately, there are in the church always a fair number of folks who take a perverse pleasure in letting you know that you in fact don't please them.

Jesus never intended us to be imprisoned by the narrow confines of others' opinions. His call to discipleship is a call to freedom, as we are released to move beyond past experiences, present obstacles, and future fears. We are called to demonstrate the Holy Spirit's enabling power in every area of our lives.

When do you know that you've finally arrived? Do you ever reach a point where you can say you have done it all, and rest in the warm glow of your accomplishments? When do you finally stop?

Some people stop when they have experienced a big failure or setback. "Why not just give up," they think. "The obstacles are too great; I can't make a difference anyway. Everyone is against me, so I may as well quit." Maybe this is how Elijah felt when, following his greatest victory, he was threatened by a corrupt queen. In fear of his life, he ran until, overwhelmed with exhaustion and despair, he fell into a suicidal depression and prayed that God would let him die.

Some people give up before they begin. It is easier to find a diversionary path, a shortcut; or they derail themselves before they ever start out. Maybe the cost seems too high, or the road too rocky, so "Why bother?" they tell themselves. Still others stop after they have experienced a bit of success.

When is enough, enough? When do we ever get to the place where we say the task is completed? Can we, like Paul, say, "I have fought the good fight, I have finished the race, I have kept the faith" (II Tim. 4:7 NIV)?

It has been said that "the test of a person's character is not at the point of failure, but at the moment of success." I don't know why it is, but most of us can be heroes when we hurt or experience the worst that life has to offer. It's harder to be men and women of character when we are successful. Maybe that's why it can be so dangerous to feel as if we have finally arrived.

One of history's great warrior/leaders was Joshua. He was a model of uncompromising conviction who led the people of Israel into their promised land. He overcame great obstacles, and enabled the people to do more than they thought humanly possible. Leading, guiding, motivating, and strategizing, he had done it all. Or so it seemed.

If anyone had a right to feel self-confident and smug about his accomplishments, it was probably Joshua. He had stood beside Moses through all the trials and tribulations of leading the people through the wilderness. Then at Moses' passing, he had led the people of Israel into the land that had been promised them, conquering city after city. He established the nation with integrity and passion, seeking to fulfill the commitments he had made to God and to the people.

In fact, he was so successful that the twelfth chapter of the book of Joshua ends with a litany to his victories. He had conquered thirty-one kings in all! Quite an accomplishment.

If ever someone deserved a comfortable pension and retirement in the sunny valley home for conquerors, it was Joshua. He had earned a much-needed rest. Yet I was surprised to find in Joshua 13:1 these words: "When Joshua was old and well advanced in years, the Lord said to him, 'You are old, and there is more land yet to conquer.' " Then as if to add insult to injury, the Lord began to list all the land that was still out there waiting to be possessed.

Living Without an Excuse

We each have things in our lives that at first glance disqualify us from further action. When I turned eighteen, back in the days of the Vietnam War, I was called up for my draft physical. Knowing how bad my eyesight was, I was confident that I would never qualify for military duty. During the long day of waiting in lines and taking tests, it was finally time for the eye test. As I entered the room, the officer on duty asked me to remove my glasses, then instructed me to read the third line of the eye chart on the wall. "What eye chart?" I asked him.

"You pass, go on down the hall," he responded, without even looking up from his papers. Later that day while weighing in on the scales, the attendant told me that I was close to being ineligible for the draft because I weighed too little for their requirements. "If you go home and lose three pounds, you will be underweight."

I couldn't believe that I was not disqualified because of my poor eyesight. What I assumed would disqualify me from service was not a factor, and the thing that would disqualify me I had not even considered.

God knows our frame, our weakness, but He is able to work in spite of and sometimes because of our condition. Jessie Alma Edge, known as Grannie to her hometown friends, won a startling victory when she became the first woman elected to city council in her hometown of Niceville, Florida. At eighty-three, she was the oldest person in the country to win a first bid for elective office.

Her qualifications for office seemed to be that she liked to talk on the phone and she was a good cook. "I don't have any enemies," she told a reporter. "If someone gets mad at me, I just bake them a cake." During her first eight years in office, she has helped get a new hospital built, developed an alternative housing center for senior citizens, built bike paths, and spearheaded a campaign to find jobs for the town's young people.

When there was resistance to her idea for a senior center, she invited the chairman of the county commission to dinner. "I fed him chicken and dumplings and convinced him that older folks needed that home." One Florida politician was deluged with Granny's persistent phone calls. "You've got to get Jessie off me," he complained. "When she calls it's like having your grandmother twist your arm!"

Still going strong at ninety, she admits to having one problem: She finds it impossible to hear the word no. How many times do we come up against a perceived obstacle or handicap and give up rather than move forward with conviction?

Before we become prematurely satisfied or think that we may be too old, God may be telling us that there are more lands yet to conquer. Like Joshua, our apparent successes can tempt us to settle for less than God's will for our lives.

We can also become derailed by apparent failures or handicaps. When five-year-old Erin Bower saw a tube of toothpaste sitting on a counter at her local K-Mart store, she didn't know that someone had put a bomb in it. Picking it up, the bomb blew off her left hand. Major league pitcher Jim Abbott, who has dismissed the notion that because he is missing a right hand he is in any way handicapped, read about the tragedy and wrote her the following letter:

Dear Erin:

Perhaps somewhere later in your lifetime you will properly understand this letter and the feelings that go behind it. Regardless, I wanted to send something along now after being made aware of your terrible accident.

As your parents have probably told you, I was born without a right hand. That automatically made me different from the other kids I was around. But you know what? It made me different only in their eyes. You see, I figured that's what the good Lord wanted me to work with. So it was my responsibility to become as good as I could at whatever I chose to do, regardless of my handicap.

I just won my first major league game. When the final out was made, a lot of things went through my mind. I thought of my parents and all the help they provided; my brother and his support; and all of my friends along the way. The only thing, Erin, that I didn't pay attention to was my handicap. You see, it had nothing to do with anything.

You're a young lady now with a tremendous life ahead of you. Whether you want to be an athlete, a doctor, lawyer or anything else, it will be up to you, and only you, how far you go. Certainly there will be some tough times ahead, but with dedication and love of life, you'll be successful in any field you choose. I'll look forward to reading about you in the future.

Again, my best, Jim Abbott, California Angels.

When we know that we belong to a God who accepts us as we are and loves us unreservedly, we are free to live without compromising our convictions. We are free to move forward in life and relationships, in spite of our apparent shortcomings. Our age, whether too old or too young, our physical attributes or emotional handicaps, and our social standing are all irrelevant. Our Lord wants to take us just as we are and grow us into all we were meant to be.

CHAPTER SIXTEEN

Unlimited
Resources

*"T*HERE must be more to life than having everything," Maurice Sendak observed. While this is true, we can find ourselves caught in the trap of thinking we don't have enough to live fully. Unable to realize the unlimited resources that are available, we are left with a grumbling discontent and unease.

When it comes to limitations in our lives, we balk, thinking that there must be something we can do to make a difference. Sometimes we mistakenly assume that God is the one holding us back, so we try to solve problems on our own terms.

I saw an article in the Seattle newspaper about cable television mogul Ted Turner. It seems that he has come up with the "Ted Commandments" to replace the biblical Ten Commandments. "Ted Turner declared the Ten Commandments obsolete yesterday," the article said.

> He also mentioned that he would pay hard cash for a happy way to end the world. Turner, who is the chairman of Turner Broadcasting, and owns CNN, as well as two Sports franchises in Atlanta, told the National Newspaper Association in Atlanta that the Biblical Ten Commandments don't relate any longer to today's world problems. When Moses went up on the mountain, there were no nuclear weapons, there was no poverty. Today the Ten Commandments just don't go over.

Instead, he has come up with ten rules of his own, which would, among other things, require that people love and respect Planet Earth and outlaw families with more than two children. He also promises to pay $500,000 to whoever comes up with the best way to end the world. Turner also mentioned that he got into broadcasting as a lark. "I did it mainly as an adventure, but now I am the king of broadcasting."

Though Ted Turner's remarks seem extreme and a little presumptuous, they reflect a growing desire in each of us to push against biblical limits and make up our own rules. Perhaps one of the characteristics of sin is the desire within us to be king of our world. We scoff at Turner for his new commandments because he, and thus his folly, is more visible. But his presumptuousness is not that different from what we exhibit every day.

We don't like limits because they seem uncomfortably restrictive to us. Instead, we set aside God's Word when it becomes uncomfortable for us. Then we establish our own standards based on what we feel is important at the moment.

Perhaps as little children we didn't want to hear our parents say no. Now as adults we don't like to hear no. In fact, it has been said that the one word an addict resists most is no. We don't like to listen to anyone who says that we have to limit ourselves or stop expressing ourselves.

Somewhere we have gotten the distorted view that it is God who holds us back in our quest for freedom and self-expression. He is perceived as the one who binds or puts limits on us. We mistakenly think that if we could just eliminate God, we would do a lot better. Unfortunately, we begin portraying Him as an angry, restrictive parent figure who withholds from us what we need.

Our view of God isn't far from that of the thirteen-year-old in Lenexa, Kansas, who recently invented what he calls "Portable Dad." When you pull the string, a boxing glove hits you in the face, and when you release it, a boot kicks you. This science project is designed to be carried with you wherever you go, so that an imaginary parent figure will remind you that there are limits.

God is not our Portable Dad. We have twisted and distorted how God relates to us. He is in fact committed to our living unlimited lives equipped by His unlimited resources. His desire is that we be released by the power of His Spirit, even though the world around us continues to be bound up. What at first may look like freedom in this world has short-term results that lead to bondage. On the other hand, the very thing that may appear to be bondage in the near term may end up being freeing. God's intention is wholeness, as we experience all that life has to offer.

Deep within us lies that longing for a life without boundaries and limitations. Being a fan of old Western movies, I remember watching the cowboys sing songs like "Don't Fence Me In." It gave me a longing for life without limits.

Another place where we experience the frustration of limits being imposed on us is our relationships with other people. Unfortunately, for most of us life is filled with people who are quick to remind us that we don't have what it takes, that we aren't measuring up to their expectations, and that we probably don't have enough resources to accomplish our dreams. Hearing this, some of us look to blame others.

Looking at others, we mistakenly assume that they are the reason we feel bound up and inhibited. We see the co-worker who was promoted above us and think that she is the reason we're not fulfilled in our job. It's easy to assume that the boss who holds us back or the supervisor who withholds affirmation and acknowledgement is the cause of our difficulties.

In our families we can blame the spouse who ignores our brilliant ideas or is unimpressed with our relational skills. There are also the family members who remind us that we aren't as great as we think we are. Some of us have aging parents or younger children who drain our energy with their incessant demands and complaints and whom we may blame for the lack of freedom and creativity in our lives. We foolishly think that if they weren't in the way, we'd be free.

A third place we experience frustration is more personal. Many people too readily blame themselves. "I have met the enemy, and he is me" becomes our self-accusing motto. Our inner

fears and doubts, insecurities and past failures, loom in our con-
sciousness to remind us that we will never accomplish anything.
Our acute awareness of limitations causes us to turn inward,
until we slide into the downward spiral of in-turned vision. Our
world grows increasingly smaller, until we can't imagine what we
would do if we had unlimited resources.

The pathway to freedom doesn't lie in blaming others or in
blaming ourselves and turning inward. Neither does it lie in as-
serting our will against God, discarding His word along the way.
The secret is in allowing Jesus Christ to empower us as we receive His unlimited resources.

The Resource of Attitude

When we think of resources available to us, it is easy to focus on
those things that are tangible and within our grasp. Some of our
most important resources are only discovered as we look within
ourselves. How we view the resources available to us can greatly
affect how we use them. Our attitude can be either a stepping-
stone to growth or a stumbling block that holds us back.

During the early years of my marriage, I was a scrooge when
it came to handling money. Unconsiously, I let money (and the
lack of it) control me. Whenever I wanted to do something, I
was able to find the way, even if it meant sacrificing in other
areas. But if my wife wanted to do something that I was not
excited about, I could justify my position by pointing out that
we simply didn't have the money.

This oppressive attitude dominated our marriage until I was
finally confronted by a friend who told me that "money is always
an excuse and never a reason." My attitude was hurting my marriage. When I realized this, we stopped fighting about money
and began dealing with the tougher underlying issues of power,
control, and ego.

Unfortunately, we in the church can also hide behind the
mask of limited resources. There is never enough money, time,
people, or energy to accomplish what needs to be done. It is easy

to use the lack of money or other resources as an excuse to cover the fear of taking risks or being out of control.

It has been said that "there is never enough money, and money is never enough." Our problems are not solely due to lack of money, nor can they be completely solved by getting more money. A larger problem is that we have not learned to have big dreams. We seem to have lost the ability to dream what God wants to do in us, in our cities, and in our world. Instead, we attempt to tell God what to do.

On the other hand, when we act as if our resources are unlimited, we become free to grow, change, and accept challenges that might at first glance seem too big for us. In other words, we allow ourselves to be thrust into situations where we must rely on God in order to survive.

Under the pretense of stewardship, we have overcontrolled our ministries. We allow the bean counters to determine our dreams for ministry, rather than letting the people with vision determine our direction. Only when we stop assuming that our resources are limited can we begin to move forward in faith.

We unwittingly squelch people's dreams for ministry because we don't think there is enough money (or time, volunteers, meeting space, etc.). We develop very logical reasons why things won't work, why the dreams will die. But we have in the process taught one another not to step out in faith or have big dreams.

It's healthy to acknowledge that there probably won't be enough money, time, people, or space to do all that we feel called to accomplish. But we can begin acting on what we do have, believing that God will provide as we have need.

I once considered myself a dreamer of big dreams, until someone challenged me to put *his* money where *my* mouth was. Mike was a young Christian who was discovering the adventure of following Christ on a daily basis. "I want to help make some of your ministry dreams come true," he mentioned. "Please let me know if you need any money to tackle a new project."

I thanked him for his generous offer and put it out of my mind until a few days later when the finance office of the church called to tell me that a very large donation had been sent to the church with the instructions, "This is for John's ministry dreams." I sent Mike a note of thanks and waited until a worthy project came along that required special funding.

One year later Mike and I were again at lunch, when he got a confused look on his face and asked me if he had insulted or offended me by sending the money the year before. I assured him that I was not offended. In fact, I had felt flattered that he trusted me with such a large amount of money.

"Then why haven't you spent it yet?" he asked.

"I'm waiting for something special," was my reply. "I want to find just the right ministry, so that I can be sure that the money is used wisely."

"Please use it," he said. "I don't care if you hand out twenty-dollar bills on the street corner. I want you to use it up so that I can have the fun of giving more."

Suddenly I realized that I was the problem. I had let myself become immobilized because I didn't want to lose the money. It was I who was the bottleneck, holding back the blessings that God intended to release. "Use it or lose it" is an old adage that applies to God's generous resources. Stewardship involves the use of God's gifts, not the hoarding of them. As I went out and used the money, I was surprised at how fun it can be to bless others with some of our unlimited resources.

If we'll begin to share our dreams for ministry, we will discover that there is more than enough to accomplish what God wants to do. Instinctively, we think of ourselves as managers or stewards of "limited resources." But in God's Kingdom the challenge is to be stewards of unlimited resources. We don't have to be practical or sensible anymore. We don't have to talk one another out of big dreams for ministry. It's fun just being a conduit of blessing: receiving and giving freely as God pours out His unlimited resources on us.

The Resource of Prayer

Prayer is one of the unlimited resources available to each of us. In this bound-up world, prayer may be a lost art, but it is always the starting point when we move toward God. In prayer we set aside our agendas, letting God's priorities become our priorities, and we receive His resources.

Amazing things happen to us when we commit to pray. Matt was sitting in the last row of the balcony while I was interviewing Tom, a friend of his, about the power of prayer. Matt told me that he had come to church that morning planning to be disruptive in order to distract Tom while he was sharing. "I thought it would be fun to get him confused and flustered so he wouldn't know what to share," he said. "I was standing in the back, waving my arms and making faces, when it hit me that Tom really meant what he was saying about believing God works through our prayers."

"I've never prayed before, but if Tom believes it, I should at least give it a try," he went on to tell me. "There were four areas of my life that had been bothering me for months, and seemed unresolvable, so I wrote them down and committed to pray each day to see what happened." Within three weeks he had received clear resolution in each of the four areas. "I guess if God can reach people like me in the balcony," Matt concluded, "He can reach anyone!"

Prayer is one of the keys that unlocks us to receive God's power. If we are feeling powerless or bound up, we must resist the urge to take immediate action and begin by asking God what He would like to happen in us.

Bruce and Gaye related their experience after signing up to participate in a twenty-four hour prayer vigil at their church. "We set the alarm for 3:30 A.M. to get ready for the 4:30 time slot that we had agreed to set aside for prayer. We woke up, showered, dressed, and drove across town to the church, only to discover that the building was locked securely for the night." (They had missed the small print encouraging people to pray at home). "We stood outside in the dark, knocking on the door, wondering how we could honor our commitment with the church closed."

"Then we got an idea," Gaye said excitedly. "We held hands and walked around the building seven times, in the dark of night, praying. Getting back into the car, we drove home, agreeing that it was one of the greatest times we had spent together."

How would you have handled that same situation? First of all, I doubt if I would have signed up for a 4:30 A.M. time commitment. But if I had come at that hour, I probably would have banged on the door for a while, been frustrated that the instructions were unclear about the church being open or closed during certain hours, and driven home angry and resentful about having ruined a good night's sleep. I probably would have returned home defeated by the obstacles that loomed before me.

Notice the difference in attitude. One says, "God brought us here at this time of the night for a reason. We came to pray; it doesn't matter whether the church is open or closed. Let's just do it." Another says, "Accept defeat when circumstances don't meet your expectations." It's easy, when confronted with roadblocks, to use the obstacles as excuses for our own unfaithfulness.

Rather than seeing ourselves surrounded by obstacles, we need to surround our obstacles with prayer. We can align ourselves with God in such a way that we gain a fresh perspective. In prayer, we have freedom to ask the Lord what He wants to do about our situation. As we surround our obstacles with prayer, watching them lose their power over us, we are set free.

The Resource of Inner Strength

There is a need to be strengthened in our inner selves. We spend a lot of time, effort, and money strengthening our outer selves. We work on our appearance, striving to have the right look, the right talk and style, in order to impress others around us. Unfortunately, we spend lots of time working on the exterior while neglecting the important task of strengthening the inner person.

Paul writes in Ephesians 3:16 that we need to be strengthened in our inner selves. This strengthening goes beyond merely improving ourselves on our own means. It's not enough to strategize, set goals, and work hard. We need God's help to strengthen our inner selves. It is only as Christ dwells in us that we become strong enough to face the obstacles.

Lloyd Ogilvie compares our lives to beautifully sculpted bonsai trees. These plants are trimmed and carefully groomed in such a way that they have the look of age and strength, while maintaining a miniature size. By trimming the roots bonsai gardeners can control the physical growth of the plants.

One of the characteristics of many Christians today is that our spiritual roots do not go deep into our relationship with Christ. Lacking spiritual rootedness, we aren't strong in our inner person. This makes us, in effect, bonsai Christians. We may have the look and appearance of maturity on the outside, but we remain stunted in our growth on the inside. We're like tiny imitations of the real thing. If we don't allow our roots to go deep in Christ, we will lack power to understand and experience God's love in its fullness.

The Resource of Relationships

Paul's prayer for the early Christians was "that you might have *power together* with all the saints" (NIV) [emphasis mine]. We get into difficulty when we try to have power alone. Jesus promised, "For where two or three are gathered in my name, there I am in the midst of them" (Matt. 18:20 RSV). Coming together in Christian community, we often find God doing more than we expected.

Results greater than the sum of the parts are obtained through involvement with others. This is why even the most creative programs in a church are really nothing more than an excuse for people to get together and minister to one another. When we are together, whether in worship, small groups, or service projects, God is present, working in and through us in surprising ways.

It is not always easy to become personally involved with other people. It can in fact be very threatening. We may feel uneasy when barriers begin to fall and unlimited resources get unleashed.

Phil Smart, a very successful businessperson, told me about an exciting plan to link business executives together. "As president of the downtown Rotary club, I am determined to move us away from being a mere check-writing club. We need to take our motto seriously and get involved personally serving the community 'one to one.' " He had come to realize that money alone can never solve the incredible problems in our city. But people linked together in committed relationships would be an unstoppable force for good.

He developed a strategy called "the Third Eight." Looking at our days in blocks of time, everyone has eight hours to sleep, eight hours to work, and eight hours of discretionary time. Phil encouraged his fellow business executives to get involved and make a difference by using their "third eight" hours of time. Soon hundreds of men and women were involved volunteering in hospitals, shelters, schools, and prisons, helping and caring in creative ways.

Though his efforts were incredibly successful, he seemed disappointed that some people resisted the challenge to personal involvement. I wasn't surprised. After all, he was asking people to step outside of the private and controlled environments they had worked so hard to build, in order to make a difference. Why wouldn't there be resistance?

Phil's challenge in the city is really no different from the challenge facing the church. We seek to mobilize ourselves in order to get face to face with real people who have real needs. Then we can be the catalysts who unleash God's unlimited resources in our needy world. The healing begins when we take the first steps of sitting down together and sharing our own needs as well as our dreams for ministry. Then we can encourage and support one another in the fulfilment of those dreams.

I know how difficult this can be, because I am not naturally a people person. There are times when I have to practically force myself to be vulnerable in small groups. I'm coming to realize that sharing in community is like using mouthwash; we do it because we need to, not because we necessarily like it. But as we meet together in vulnerable, accountable relationships, God's unlimited resources are unleashed, and we are set free to live beyond the limits of our own lives.

PART V

The Big
Picture

CHAPTER SEVENTEEN

Unfinished Masterpiece

*N*O one wants to miss the big picture. We don't want to get so caught up in the mundane details all around us that we overlook the truly important events. Neither do we want the trivial to cause us to miss out on the most significant.

I'm a movie fan and have been known to frequent movie theaters on more than an occasional basis. I usually go in search of that special blockbuster movie, the big picture that will really make an impression. I seek the advice of wiser, more experienced movie goers to help me pick which movies to see. I found that movie ads are a great source of valuable information. They tell us everything we want to know, and they do it in grand style.

Lately, I've come to see that the movie ads are saying less and less in bigger and bigger ways. I came across some "exciting but meaningless movie blurbs" in my son's *Mad Magazine*. These caught the spirit of many of our movie ads: "Filmed completely in its entirety"; "You'll laugh until you stop"; "From the makers of a previous film, comes another one"; "Every once in a while a film comes along; this is such a film"; "One of the year's most recent movies"; "This movie will have you in the middle of your seat, with your back against the chair, and your elbows on the armrests"; "If this is the kind of film you like, then this is the film for you."

What is true in advertising is also true in the rest of our lives. We get bombarded with promises and promotional material that make extravagant claims but too often leave us empty and disappointed, thinking that we have surely missed something. We need more than ever to find the big picture in our lives, to find something of content and value that will make a difference.

It is critical for us to understand what is most important in life. We need to find the non-negotiables, the anchors that help us make sense of life, that keep us from drifting around with the currents.

Weathervane Christians

While visiting in New England, I was impressed with the beauty and variety of their weathervanes. Driving along country roads, it's not unusual to see old weathervanes above the homes and barns. Designs that included a variety of farm animals were turning faithfully in the wind, pointing out the direction of every gust and breeze.

As I watched them turn, I pictured in my mind's eye how very much like weathervanes we can become in our lives. It is easy to break loose of God's absolutes and lose our bearings. Without rootedness we can be continually turned around by society's winds. Sensitive to pressure from friends, family, and culture, we find ourselves spinning according to the pressure of the day. If we cease to be men and women of commitment, we will lack the strength to stand in the face of pressure, instead choosing to move more and more according to our impulses. Let's consider some of the anchors that give our lives stability.

Identity Anchors

Some people find traditions to be the anchor for their lives. They give us a sense of rootedness, a quiet confidence that everything is all right, in its place and predictable. Some young families are discovering that they can start their own new traditions, to help them feel connected or rooted.

Some traditions are very positive. They remind us of who we are and give predictability to special events. Negative experiences however, can also turn into a form of tradition as well.

In my family, we had a negative tradition around Christmas each year: the annual "setting up the Christmas tree" fight. We would go out to shop for a tree, but we never could agree on the size, shape, or style of tree to buy. I usually was drawn to the cheap Charlie Brown type of trees, which I'd feel sorry for. Eileen liked the grand, gigantic, elegant trees. We fought over buying the tree. Then we fought about how to tie it on the car to drive it home. We fought about hauling it into the house and setting it up. We fought about whether to use the water basin holders or the crossed boards as a stand. We argued and struggled each step of the way.

The day came when we decided to start a new tradition. Now, every year Eileen and our son Damian go out and select a tree, tie it on to the car, drive it home, haul it into the house, set it up, and decorate it. Then I come home from work and say, "That's nice." It's a new tradition!

Traditions give our lives a sense of structure that helps to reduce our anxieties. They also provide a sense of meaning. Holiday activities, family, and community practices give vitality to the special events of life.

In the same way that traditions help to define who we are, some of us choose to define ourselves in other ways. For example, a job can also provide our identity, an identity that lasts only as long as we have the job. If we are laid off, then we struggle with our identity and wonder if we are valued. I'm convinced that our tendency toward workaholism is grounded in our fear that outside of the workplace we won't have an identity. In the office we know who we are, what's expected, and how well we measure up.

Others may get their identity from their place in the family. Families can give us that sense of security and identity. As long as the family structure is in order, we all know what part we play, whether the bright, gifted one or the rowdy problem person. We know our place and play out the roles that reinforce and validate our lives.

Some people find their value from their place in the church. We may not have much power anywhere else in our life, but when we come to church, we feel strong, competent, and in control. We focus our time and energy on the church. Serving on committees and task forces too often leads to further commitments, until every night is spent in church involvements. Church work consumes us to the point that we begin to lose balance and perspective. Even pastors aren't immune to this disease of blurred focus and burn-out.

Families, traditions, jobs, church—all are helpful in bringing stability to us. They can help provide a sense of meaning, place, and value in our lives, but they aren't the most important anchor.

In John, the Gospel writer calls us back to the basics. "In the beginning was the Word . . . and the Word was God. . . . In him was life, and that life was the light of [the world]" (John 1:1–4 NIV). In what is our life grounded? Is it in Christ? Or is it wrapped up in how we appear, or in what we think others think of us? Is it in what we have, or whom we know? Is our life a collection of all the trophies we've collected along the way? Is it in what we have done, or where we have been? Or is it rooted and grounded in Him who is life?

The lesser things are not the most important legacy that we can leave behind. Everyone leaves some kind of tracks. Some of us try to sneak by without leaving very big impressions in the sand. Hoping to get by without being discovered, we live with whispers and hushed tones. We spend our energy covering up and cleaning up so that no one will ever know where we have been.

Others may be more obvious, like the "Peanuts" character Pigpen. Wherever he goes, a huge cloud of dust swirls behind him. We can also move along unmindful of the swirling mess that we are leaving for others to clean up.

Either way, the kind of tracks we leave behind are a reflection of what is most important to us. However, there really is only one thing that is important. Compared to knowing Christ, everything else is peripheral. Do we know Him who gives life? Will we walk in the light that He brings into our dark world? Will our life be a dusty, half-empty shelf where we display the evidence that we have been here? This is our choice.

Until we get to the point where we say yes to Jesus Christ on a daily basis and allow Him to be the source of our light and life, everything else is out of alignment, really doesn't matter.

Until we allow Christ's power and presence to break through our defenses in a radical way, we will continue to struggle along on our own limited resources and energy.

Until we set aside our private excuses and personal agendas and allow this radical relationship with Christ to permeate our lives, relationships, families, work, and, yes, even churches, we will miss the big picture that in Him is life and that life is the light of the world.

The Gospel of John goes on to point out that "the light shines in the darkness, and the darkness has not overcome it" (John 1:5 RSV). Getting the big picture helps us realize that every person who has a personal relationship with Christ has His life and light in them. Therefore, they will not be overcome with the darkness of our world.

Do you ever feel overcome by the pressures in your life? I sure do. Do you ever sense that there isn't enough time, money, resources, or strength to merely survive another day? That you are just hanging on? The expectations that other people have for you pile up and scream out their reminder that you are not adequate, capable, or perfect enough to succeed.

So we either dig in and try harder or fall back in defeat and give up the struggle. We don't feel very much like overcomers. We wonder if perhaps we are missing something. And life goes by. We lose a sense of what is really important.

In the story *The Little Prince*, the prince said, "I know a planet where there is a certain red-faced gentleman. He has never smelled a flower. He has never looked at a star. He has never loved anyone. He's never done anything in his life, but add up figures. All day he says over and over, 'I'm busy with matters of consequence.' And that makes him swell up with pride. But, he is not a man, he is a mushroom."

When we allow ourselves to become caught up in minuscule battles, fixed on adding up our figures, and on the little issues all around us, we lose sight of the big picture. We feel our light growing dim, and as if we don't have what it takes to make it through another day. We think there must be something wrong with us. We should have been victorious. We should be happy and capable. Because we aren't, we must not have what it takes to follow Christ. But wait. "To all who received Him, who believed in His name, he gave power to become children of God."

What is the power for? The Bible doesn't say it is the power to get rich. Nor is it power to have wonderful children, or never to have to worry again. It isn't even power to love your job, feel excited about your church, never be depressed or lonely or grieve when someone you love dies or tragedy happens in the world. That isn't what the power is for.

As long as we live, there will be disappointment and sin. But in the midst of all the darkness, we will not be overcome because we have been given the power to be children of God. This means first of all that we are His. We are known and loved by Him; we have access to God because of our intimate relationship with Him.

Second, it means we are not "only" children (much as many of us would like to be). We belong to a family not of our choosing, one with all the quirks and eccentricities of a natural family. You are drawn into a fellowship of people who are not exactly like you—God's family.

Having the power to be a child of God gives us the freedom to dare to take care of others in the family. We can share our struggles and doubts, supporting others and encouraging them. It means that what happens in our lives and relationships matters. It means we are not alone. It means that whatever happens to us, we know who we are and whose we are. We know that we are part of God's family, that we are the object of His deepest love and attention, and that there is nothing more important to Him than us. His power enables us to overcome the dark spots in our lives. He gives us the courage to move out in spite of ourselves.

Finally, it means being the church. This is a lot more than being part of a social club or service agency. The church is more than a pit stop we pull into along the road of life. It's not the place to get a refill of inspiration or energy, or where we get directions before zooming off on our own power, going our own way. The church is where we discover the power to be God's family together, where dreams for ministry are nurtured, watered, and encouraged. This is where responsibilities are shared, where everyone has a part to play, and we are strengthened and healed. Here we prepare to go out and face spiritual warfare; we are equipped with power and deployed in the world.

Bars of Hope

Driving through the streets of Mexico City one day, I was intrigued by the large number of homes that had long metal bars rising up above their roofs. Looking over the city, there are thousands of buildings large and small that have steel bars rising above them. I asked the driver to explain the metal sticking up from the homes. He said that they are called *barras de esperanza*, which translates "bars of hope."

"When families build their homes," he said, "they often don't have the money or resources to complete the project. Perhaps they don't know how large of a family they will have. So they take what they have and begin the project. When they have completed as much as possible, they leave the structural bars rising up above the home as a visible symbol for their neighbors and anyone who happens to pass by the house, saying, 'We are not finished with this house yet.' These are bars of hope to remind us that we are still building, to demonstrate that there is more to come."

Paul writes in Philippians, "I am confident that he who began a good work in you will bring it to completion on the day of Jesus Christ." God is not finished with us yet. The beams of the empty cross are our bars of hope. They are visible symbols of what He wants to do in us as he brings His work to fulfillment.

The greatest work of an artist is called the masterpiece. It is the visible demonstration of the creator's finest handiwork. When God first thought of you, He envisioned your life and set out to create the marvelous, unique person that you are. God has begun a good work in you, and each day that you follow Him in the steps of discipleship, you will discover anew that He will complete the masterpiece.

This is an extension of the copyright page.

Taken from a "Dear Abby" column, © 1989 by Universal Press Syndicate. Reprinted with permission.

Cathy, © 1991 by Cathy Guisewhite. Reprinted with permission of Universal Press Syndicate.

Excerpt from *The Addictive Organization*, by Anne Wilson Schaef and Diane Fassel. © 1988 by Anne Wilson Schaef and Diane Fassel. Reprinted by permission of HarperCollins Publishers.

Another Fun-O-Rama® Design. © 1987 by Matt Groening and Steve Vance. All rights reserved.

"Reasons I Cheat," by Randy Travis, © 1987 by Sometimes You Win Music. All rights reserved. Used by permission.

Excerpt from *The Alexander Complex*, © 1989 by Michael Meyer. Reprinted by permission of Random House, Inc.

Excerpt from "Exciting but Meaningless Movie Studio Blurbs," by Russ Cooper, from the January 1990 issue of *Mad Magazine*, © 1989 by E. C. Publications Inc.

Letter from Jim Abbott, taken from "Abbott's best example to kids is being himself," bylined Art Thiel, from the *Seattle Post-Intelligencer*. Reprinted courtesy of the *Seattle Post-Intelligencer*.

Excerpt from "House destroyer cleared of assault against cameraman," by Ed Penhale, March 1, 1986, from the *Seattle Post-Intelligencer*. Reprinted courtesy of the *Seattle Post-Intelligencer*.

"I Saw the Lord" by Dallas Holm, © 1981 by Dimension Music and Going Holm. Used by permission.